SOCIAL CONFLICT IN PRISON ORGANIZATION

by

George Sherman Rothbart

A Dissertation

Doctor of Philosophy

UNIVERSITY OF WASHINGTON

1964

REPRINTED IN 1975 BY

R AND E RESEARCH ASSOCIATES

4843 MISSION STREET, SAN FRANCISCO 94112

18581 McFARLAND AVE., SARATOGA, CALIFORNIA 95070

PUBLISHERS AND DISTRIBUTORS OF ETHNIC STUDIES

EDITOR: ADAM S. ETEROVICH

PUBLISHER: ROBERT D. REED

LIBRARY OF CONGRESS CARD CATALOG NUMBER

74-29580

ISBN

0-88247-316-6

ACKNOWLEDGEMENTS

My major debt of gratitude for help and encouragement in the design and prosecution of this study is owed to Dr. Clarence C. Schrag. Dr. Schrag was responsible for my developing an interest in correctional organization and has provided great intellectual stimulation and guidance in this work. Dr. Herbert Costner was both co-worker and counselor in carrying out the work of analyzing the data, and much of the success of the research operation bears his stamp.

Numerous persons have provided important help. The members of Dr. Schrag's seminar made many useful suggestions regarding questionnaire construction. Mr. Rodolfo Alvarez was working along somewhat similar lines and contributed a number of valuable comments. Mr. David R. Straub provided a great deal of painstaking help in processing the questionnaire data. Dr. William S. Robinson and Dr. Ted T. Jitodai, of the University of Oregon, provided valuable advice.

Special thanks are owed to the inmates of Western State Reformatory. Although they were paid for participation, the rewards were small and most of these men put up with the inconvenience because of a genuine desire to help in this kind of research. The staff of the Reformatory, correctional officers, administrators, caseworks, all went to great lengths to make our study a success.

Finally, acknowledgement is made to the Ford Foundation and to the Research Computer Laboratory of the University of Washington. Grants from both agencies provided for the costs of carrying out the research.

TABLE OF CONTENTS

CHAPTER		PAGE
I.	THE PRISON AND THE STUDY OF CONFLICT	1
	Introduction	1
	The problem of This Study	2
	Use of the Prison in This Study	2
	Approaches to the Study of Conflict	3
	Cultural dissensus approaches to conflict	3
	The rational or interest approach to conflict	6
	The functional school of conflict	10
	Process approaches to conflict	10
II.	A SOCIAL-PSYCHOLOGICAL THEORY OF CONFLICT	16
	A Definition	16
	Some Basic Terms	19
	Some Basic Propositions	20
	Dominance and conflict	20
	Dominance and threat	23
	Status threat	25
	Control and exchange	25
	Dominance and mock behavior	26
	Dominance and withdrawal behavior	27
	Dominance and the perceived sources of action	28
	Dominance, exchange, and the perceived sources of action	29
	Negotiated reward as a style of life	29
III.	THE INTERPERSONAL ENVIRONMENT AND CONFLICT	34
	The Effects of Culture on Conflict	34
	The Informational Aspects of the Social Milieu	34
	The Social Milieu Can Provide an Audience	36
	What is the Effect of Conflict on the Social Milieu	37
	Summary of the Theory of Conflict	38

CHAPTER		PAGE
IV.	THE RESEARCH DESIGN	40

    The Setting   40
    The Sample   41
        Drawing the initial sample   42
        Characteristics of the sample   43
    Questionnaire Administration   48
    The Instruments Used in the Questionnaire   49
    The Characteristics of the Instruments   50
        Protest   50
        Sympathy   50
        Reward   51
        Friendship   51
        Self-type   53
        Instrumentalism   53
        Personalism   54
    Statistical Techniques Used in the Study   55

| V. | THE MEANING OF PROTEST | 58 |

    The Relationship between Conflict and Protest   58
    Development of the Scale   58
    The Characteristics of Selected Items   61
    Protest and Its Objects   63
    Protest and Violation of Institutional Rules   63
    Conformity to Staff Expectations and Rule Violations   66
    Protest and Inmate Assault   67
    Protest and Conflict: A Summary   67

| VI. | THE COGNITIVE WORLD OF THE PROTESTOR | 70 |

    Exchange Balance and Protest   70
    The Personal Qualities of Staff and Inmates and Protest   74
    Personalism and Protest   77
    Social Types and Protest   78
    Social Types and Instrumentalism   82
    Summary   84

| VII. | THE STRUCTURAL CORRELATES OF PROTEST | 86 |

    Social Structure and Conflict   86
    Previous Criminal Experiences and Protest   86
    Status and Protest   87
    Informal Social Relations and Protest   89
    Friends' Social Type and Protest   90
    A Test of the Audience Effect   91

CHAPTER		PAGE
	Time Served and Protest	93
	Personalism, Time Served, and Protest	95
	Summary	97
VIII.	METHODOLOGICAL PROBLEMS IN THE ANALYSIS OF CHANGE	99
	The Problem of Differential Scale Variance	99
	The Problem of Regression toward the Mean	100
	Computation of Regressed Scores	101
IX.	ANALYSIS OF CHANGE: SOME SELECTED FINDINGS	103
	Personalism and Change	103
	Work Crew Status and Change	105
	The Selectivity of Reward	108
	Self-Friends Matrix and Change	109
	Instrumentalism and Change	111
	Social Type and Protest	112
X.	ANALYSIS OF CHANGE: EXCHANGE BALANCE	116
	Theories of Exchange Balance	116
	Three Alternative Hypotheses	116
	A Test of the Exchange Balance Hypothesis	118
	The Limited Effect of Exchange Imbalance	119
	Changes Related to Exchange Imbalance	120
	A Conclusion	121
XI.	AN EXPLORATORY EXPERIMENT	125
	The Experimental Design	126
	Manipulation of the Stimulus Variables	126
	The Experimental Results	127
XII.	SUMMARY AND CONCLUSIONS	131
	The Propositions	131
	The Findings	132
	The characteristics and consequences of protest	132
	Perception of staff	133
	Perception of inmates	133
	Perception of self	133
	Negotiated Reward	133
	Social structure	134
	Protest versus sympathy	134

CHAPTER	PAGE
BIBLIOGRAPHY	136
APPENDIX A. LETTER OF SOLICITATION TO INMATES	141
APPENDIX B. THE QUESTIONNAIRE INSTRUMENTS	142
Instruments Using Likert-Type Format	142
Friends' Type Scale	146
Instrumentalism Scale	148
The Personalism Scale	150
The Semantic Differentials	153
The Social Background Items	154
The "Wheeler" Conformity Items	156
The Work Crew Status Scale	158
APPENDIX C. THE REGRESSED SCORES AND CUTTING POINTS	161
Calculation of Regressed Protest Scores	161
Cutting Points for Protest and Sympathy Scores	162

LIST OF TABLES

TABLE		PAGE
I.	Percent of Inmates Who Volunteered for Panel	44
II.	Rate of Continued Participation of Inmates Who Volunteered for Panel	44
III.	Time Served by Respondent and Non-Respondent Groups as of September 1, 1962	46
IV.	Percent of Respondent and Non-Respondent Groups Who Had No Rule Violations (September 1, 1962)	47
V.	Mean Rate for Rule Violations per Month among Inmates who had a Rule Violation, by Respondent and Non-Respondent Groups (September 1, 1962)	48
VI.	Protest Scores of Drop-Outs and Non-Drop-Outs at Time of First Questionnaire	48
VII.	Comparison of Responses by High and Low Quartiles on Sympathy Scale to Three Items	52
VIII.	Comparison of Responses by High and Low Quartiles on Protest Scale to Three Items	60
IX.	Comparison of Responses by High and Low Quartiles on Protest Scale to Five "Specific" Items	62
X.	Semantic Differential Ratings of Custody Staff, Treatment Staff, and Inmates by Protest Quartiles	64
XI.	Relationship between Protest and Rule Infractions	66
XII.	Relationship between Conformity to Inmate Role Expectations and Rule Violations	67
XIII.	Relationship between Assault against Another Inmate and Protest	68
XIV.	Relationships between the Protest Scale and Selected Items from the Sympathy and Reward Scales	73

TABLE		PAGE
XV.	Mean Scores of Protest Quartiles on Semantic Differential	76
XVI.	Relationship of Social Types to Previous Criminal Experiences	80
XVII.	Protest Scores of Four Social Types	81
XVIII.	Social Types and Personalism	81
XIX.	Responses of Four Social Types to the Instrumentalism Scale	83
XX.	Relationship of Previous Criminal Experiences and Protest	87
XXI.	Relationship between Work Crew Status and Protest Scores	89
XXII.	Relationship between Perceived Characteristics of Friends and Protest Scores	90
XXIII.	Relationship between Self-Friends Matrix and Protest Score	92
XXIV.	Relationship between Self-Friends Matrix and Sympathy Score	93
XXV.	Relationships between Time Served and Protest and Sympathy Scores	94
XXVI.	Relationships between Institutional Career Phase and Sympathy and Protest Scores	95
XXVII.	Relationship between Time Served and Protest Scores, Controlled for Level of Personalism	96
XXVIII.	Relationship between Time Served and Sympathy Scores, Controlled for Level of Personalism	97
XXIX.	Relationship between Personalism Level and Attitude Change	103
XXX.	Relationship between Work Crew Status and Attitude Change for Those Whose Work Crew did not Change from Time One to Time Three	106
XXXI.	Relationship between Work Crew Status Change and Attitude Change	106
XXXII.	Relationship between Work Crew Status Change and Initial Protest and Sympathy Scores at Time One	109

TABLE		PAGE
XXXIII.	Relationship Between Self-Friends Matrix and Attitude Change	110
XXXIV.	Relationship Between Instrumentalism Score and Attitude Change	111
XXXV.	Relationship Between Social Type at Time Two and Protest Change	112
XXXVI.	Relationship Between Social Type at Time Three and Protest Change	114
XXXVII.	Relationship Between Protest-Sympathy Combinations and Attitude Change	119
XXXVIII.	The Relationship of Experimental Groups to Protest and Sympathy Change	128
XXXIX.	Relationship of Experimental Groups to Personalism and Personalism Change	129

LIST OF FIGURES

FIGURE		PAGE
1.	Intercorrelation Matrix of Protest, Sympathy, and Reward	71
2.	Semantic Differential Profiles of Protest Groups' Perceptions of Inmates and Custody Staff by Inmates	75
3.	Protest Versus Sympathy Scattergram	122

CHAPTER I

THE PRISON AND THE STUDY OF CONFLICT

INTRODUCTION

In the past few years the topic of conflict has come to evoke an increasing flurry of discussion, theoretical speculation, and critical review. Indeed, essays have been written to exhort sociologists to devote more attention to this area.[1] One evidence of this general trend is an academic periodical, The Journal of Conflict Resolution, which has attracted outstanding contributions in its few years of existence.

At least one interesting riddle emerges from the study of the literature on conflict. It is that empirically oriented articles on conflict seldom cite research that was explicitly designed to explore or to test propositions about conflict behavior. The usual article reports research that "brought to mind," or "was directly relevant to," conflict. Why is there a paucity of direct research?

The traditional problem of economics, marketplace behavior, has given the economist a natural interest in conflict relationships.[2] On the other hand, the fields of sociology and anthropology have typically focused on the problem of consensus, and the interest in conflict is novel.[3] In fact, sociologists have tended to treat the subject of conflict by generalizing insights gained from the study of consensus and dissensus. As we shall see, the identification of dissensus with conflict is an inadequate formulation. Thus, sociology has not had a long time to accumulate research dealing specifically with conflict situations.

Another reason for the lack of research materials is the absence of a clear differentiation between conflict and sociology's other concerns. Many sociologists may not feel that conflict needs special treatment; if this is so, time might not produce more research. For this reason, one of the aims of the present study will be to develop a clearer delimitation of the range of phenomena that can be usefully labelled "conflict behavior."

There are some outstanding exceptions to the aforementioned neglect. Some studies have recently appeared that deal with conflict behavior in the area of community relations, voting behavior, industrial relations, criminology, and corrections.[4]

THE PROBLEM OF THIS STUDY

It is the purpose of this study to add to the growing body of research on the sociology of conflict by studying behavior within the walls of a modern prison. Our central focus will be to explain differing tendencies to come into conflict with the staff, among inmates in the institution. We shall aim to develop a variety of propositions and to provide some evidence as to their validity.

USE OF THE PRISON IN THIS STUDY

Few writers on conflict make reference to the voluminous material on correctional communities; yet even a quick survey of the literature of penology indicates that conflict between staff and inmates is much of the sum and substance around which daily prison life finds its orbit. For example, at least two studies indicate that the prison is one of the special classes of institutions in which the degree of conflict between upper and lower ranked individuals is "overperceived" by both types of persons.[5] The military establishment may be another example of this type of institution.[6] Individuals in such institutions who happen to feel low antagonism toward "the other side" tend to hide their feelings, unaware that some of their fellows share their views.

One would think that such reports offer important empirical data for the study of the origins and processes of conflict. Since, by and large, the material has not been so perceived, it is useful to ask why the field of correction has been slighted.

The answer may lie in the traditional emphases that have existed in correctional research. The average criminologist is much aware of the conflict that exists in correctional settings and perhaps in consequence tends to orient himself in two different directions. The first is that of studying the nature and scope of the antagonistic inmate culture. Most prison studies confine themselves to this direction. Clemmer's definition of prisonization gives us the crux of this approach:

> ... We may use the term _prisonization_ to refer to the taking on in a greater or less degree of the folkways, mores, customs and general culture of the penitentiary.[7]

Clemmer cites the "capacity for integration into a prison-primary group"[8] as one of the important factors predicting the degree of prisonization.

The other direction in which the criminologist's interest may move, perhaps simultaneously with the first, is to ask, "How can the prison staff be legitimated to the inmates?" For example, Cressey discusses the problems of a staff which is attempting to be "helpers" and to offer treatment to the inmate group. The difficulties of such a stance are truly imposing, as he rightly points out.[9] Similarly, there is a concern with creating, among inmates, legitimacy for the larger society.

Both concerns follow from the view of social structure which maintains that consensus is that which makes social order possible. Such a view would suggest that to improve the functioning of the social order it is necessary to increase the degree of consensus that exists among the participants. As Dahrendorf says, such a view pervades most sociological thinking.[10] The prison is the very case which argues most strongly against total acceptance of the consensual point of view. The prison is a society in which, at least on the verbal level, the official elite is almost totally de-legitimated and normative consensus is at minimum. Given these obstacles, the elite often manages to achieve many of its aims and normally maintains a high degree of internal order.

Perhaps the liberal bias of many sociologists disposes them to say, in effect, "Order and control gotten without legitimacy is not to be valued." Or perhaps there is disbelief that such order is possible. At any rate, great differences in behavior -- if not in attitude -- exist among inmates. Upon parole, many leave their criminal careers behind and become reasonably law-abiding members of the society. When such transformations occur, they often occur among quite prisonized convicts, and often occur without the inmate's conferral of legitimacy to the prison staff or to the larger society. As Lipset points out, fairly stable political orders have been built out of such material.[11]

An interesting chapter in the sociology of knowledge emerges from the fact that many students of international conflict do not share this "consensual bias" and thus have more to say about the nature of "brute force" relations.[12] Since, in international conflict, the opposition cannot be expected to integrate itself into one's own social order, other solutions must be sought.

The prison, then, provides material for studying the ways in which conflict is reduced or enhanced in an order that lacks legitimacy to its lower ranked members.

APPROACHES TO THE STUDY OF CONFLICT

A review of the literature suggests several major approaches that have dominated conflict theory. Though they are all relevant to the present study, each fails to consider some crucial issues.

Cultural Dissensus Approaches to Conflict

The first type of approach explains conflict as the product of divergent group norms. We may call this perspective the "cultural dissensus" approach. In the industrial area Mayo's early work has been followed by that of many others who conclude that workers tend to develop their own production norms that conflict with those of management.[13] The notion that delinquent and criminal offenders, in general, are the product of sub-cultural norms was articulated quite early by Thrasher,[14] Sutherland,[15] and others, and still has much influence in current thinking. Miller, among others, is a modern representative of this school.[16] When proponents of the cultural dissensus school purportedly explain variations in conflict behavior among individuals or sub-groups of these respective cultural systems, they, in fact, tend to explain the process of integration into cultural systems rather than conflict as such. A good example of this tendency is found in Stanton Wheeler's work on a modern reformatory.[17]

Wheeler's major dependent variable is a scale of what he calls "conformity to staff role expectations."[18] Examination of his data shows that the staff and inmate groups endorse opposite positions on all except one of the items in the scale. Thus, we can conclude that the approximate opposite of conformity to staff role expectations is conformity to inmate role expectations. Wheeler's major findings may be summarized as follows:

1. Inmates who are low on conformity to staff role expectations (high on conformity to inmate expectations) are high on what may be called *socialization* or *prisonization* variables. That is, they have been in the institution a long time, have high contact with inmates, low contact with staff, low contact with outside persons, long criminal record, etc.

2. Inmates perceive greater disagreement with staff, relative to inmate and staff roles, than actually appears from a comparison of inmate and staff responses.

3. Staff members perceive greater disagreement with inmates, relative to inmates' roles, than actually appears from a comparison of inmate and staff responses.

If conflict can be identified with dissensus, Wheeler's scale should be related to conflict behavior, as should the socialization variables. Such a hypothesis receives some support from the work of Peter Garabedian, who studied a prison using items similar to Wheeler's as a measure of inmate conformity to staff role expectations.[19] He found rule infractions to be negatively related to conformity to staff role expectations. Furthermore, he found that as contact with inmates increases, the proclivity for rule infractions among the low-conforming inmates increases; thus this study suggests that the aforementioned socialization variables affect behavior in the anticipated direction.

McCleery and Cloward provide evidence in marked contrast to that suggested above.[20] Cloward speaks of control by the inmate social system of the more extreme forms of conflict behavior. Inmate leaders, he states, normally have a stake in maintaining a "cool" institution and will take steps to calm down the more hotheaded inmates who tend to take offense at the slightest provocation by the staff. Cloward interprets such behavior as an expression of a social norm that prescribes the maintenance of order and stability -- a norm not considered by Wheeler. In a sense, then, Cloward leaves the cultural dissensus model intact by pointing out that some norms are shared by the opposing parties. "An inmate who assaults a guard is 'fighting the system in the *wrong* way.'"[21] Certain kinds of conflict are encouraged, others prohibited.

Such a finding is consonant with many studies of restriction of production in industry, whose authors find that informal norms discourage the extreme forms of goldbricking or "chiseling" as much as they discourage "rate busting" or "job killing."[22]

McCleery addresses himself directly to the question of conflict in a study of Oahu Prison, the Hawaiian maximum security institution.[23] He studied the prison during a long period in which stability and order turned to strife and back to order again. McCleery found that different groups in the prison had quite different degrees of commitment to the "norm" of order and peace. Under the usual conditions prevailing in the traditional prison, he states, inmate leaders established covert exchange relationships with guards. Inmate leaders controlled aggressive acts by other inmates in return for certain privileges for themselves and their adherents.[24] Nonetheless, these highly adaptive leaders found it necessary to join with others in expressing contempt for officials.

At the same time that inmates appear to admire those who share the "adaptive norm" of _order_ and _stability_, high status is also accorded the more conflict-oriented inmate.

> High status was accorded those . . . who demonstrated through time a capacity to withstand the most severe sanctions bravely and without breaking. The man who retained his own initiative and capacity to do his own time in the face of the most savage punishments, maintained a standing in the inmate community equivalent to that of "bull of the yard," even in periods when he was helplessly isolated in a punishment cell.[25]

It is not clear that for McCleery's inmates the ideal of peace and order was a norm. McCleery calls it an _adaptive norm,_ but violators of this prescription are treated as semi-heroes. Clearly, some special explanation is needed of the operation of a norm when both the conformers and the extreme deviants are admired.

Even if we accept the notion that the emphasis on peace and order is a norm in prison society, in the cultural perspective we are left with problems in explaining conflict. In the first place, we find variations in the degree of conflict between staff and inmates, both over time and among various segments of the inmate population. Second, the cultural perspective offers explanation neither of the origins of the norms on which staff and inmate differ nor of the origins of those on which they agree. Wheeler offers evidence that the inmates' conception of how other inmates feel on any issue is formed largely by observing the most visible inmates. For reasons that are not entirely clear, the most visible inmates are those who are most anti-staff.[26] The inmate is guided toward anti-staff behavior by a _public_ prison culture which, at least initially, is at variance with almost everyone else's private conceptions too, but as the inmate acquires time in the institution, as well as formal and informal status, he begins to incorporate the anti-staff role. At the same time, he acquires visibility. Thus, he comes to serve as a model for the perpetuation of the culture.

Wheeler's argument is doubtless a profound insight into the mechanics of cultural transmission. But it seems somewhat tautological as an explanation of cultural origins. The tautology becomes especially clear when one considers that a reason (not offered by Wheeler) for the low visibility of pro-staff opinions is the perception that such opinions are uncommon or not acceptable. The tautology could be partially overcome by offering explanations of the finding that visible inmates tend to be more anti-staff (or in some respects pro-staff, as pointed out by McCleery and Cloward) than less visible inmates.

-5-

The Rational or Interest Approach to Conflict

A more direct approach to the problem of the origin of norms that foster or restrain conflict is made by proponents of what we shall call the rational or interest school of conflict. It is exemplified in the point of view of many economists, some sociologists, and some decision theorists. Marx, of course, portrayed the relationships between the social classes as charaterized by conflict. He saw the conflict as caused by objective divergences of interest between the classes. To Marx, in fact, the existence of social classes was an expression of the conflict of interest groups. "Individuals form a social class only insofar as they are engaged in a struggle with another class."[27]

It is a simple insight that an objective disparity between groups in the achieving of rewards from a social system has the property of producing group antagonisms. That Marx's notion has had such a delayed but profound impact -- that it comes as an insight at all -- can be explained only by the great emphasis that sociology has placed on the contrary notion that society be conceived as a system of moral norms. In contrast, Marx's view held that "the modern state is but an association that administrates the common business of the whole bourgeois class."[28] A number of sociologists, in explaining deviant behavior, have presented theories which can be called a Marxian view of deviancy. As we shall try to point out later, Marx held a more sophisticated and in many ways more useful conception of the process of development of conflict than is incorporated in modern deviancy theory.

One of the most prominent of the interest theorists is Vold, who refers to the much-noted fact that the lower classes have a higher crime rate than upper-class groups. In contrast to Sutherland's notion of a different _moral order_ existing among lower-class individuals, he states that the differential crime rate exists because the criminal law and the legal machinery are controlled by the selfish class interests of the socially dominant groups. His statement is worth quoting because it parallels Marx's last quoted statement so closely:

> The whole political process of law making, law breaking and law enforcement becomes a reflection of deep-seated and fundamental conflicts between interest groups and their more general struggles for the control of the police power of the state. Those who produce legislative majorities win control over the police power and dominate the policies that decide who is likely to be involved in a violation of the law.[29]

Modern criminological theory has moved away from Sutherland and toward Marx and Vold as represented in the works of Merton,[30] Cloward,[31] and Cohen.[32] According to Merton, objective disprivilege in a social system is correlated with the deviancy rate. But, if we look at a variety of social systems, we see great variation in the degree of correlation. This is so because individuals must be frustrated by their disprivilege in order to have a motivation to be deviant. Such frustration occurs in a system (such as our own) which indoctrinates most citizens with the same competitive aspirations. Since the lower classes are objectively disprivileged in trying to fulfill these aspirations, the lower-class person begins to reject the moral order and may actively attack it through crime, rebellion, etc. Merton combines the cultural perspective of Durkheim and the conflict perspective of Marx by viewing deviancy as a function of both moral and rational forces.[33] His commitment to society as a <u>moral collectivity</u> is suggested by the statement that the inadequate socialization of certain individuals will result in their being the "first" deviants when the aforementioned deprivation occurs. The moral order is sluggish to change; adequate socialization with respect to the moral code reduces the tendancy to deviancy even when strong forces are at work creating such deviancy. But in a perverse way, as a body of values the society creates deviancy by <u>successfully</u> socializing individuals to aspire to the success goals. Repeated frustrations may lead to conflict, deviancy, and the breakdown of moral order. Cultures must, in the long run, provide rational motives for conformity to gain and keep adherents. Note, however, that in no way does Merton see conflict as the products of competing norms. He sees conflict as the product of a sick society which has sown its own seed of dissention and has come to be faced with a host of <u>individuals</u> at war with it.

The completely rationalistic explanation of conflict and accomodation becomes appropriate, says Merton, when:

> With the resulting attenuation of institutional imperatives, there occurs an approximation of the situation erroneously held by utilitarians to be typical of societies generally wherein calculations of advantage and fear of punishment are the sole regulatory agencies.[34]

This explanation of social behavior is interesting because it suggests that in a prison, where "institutional imperatives" are certainly attenuated, punishment and reward are the principal regulatory influences. Their use, or misuse, should provide a complete explanation of conflict behavior. In this respect, Merton agrees with old-line custody-oriented prison staff. He holds that rational differences of interest explain tendencies to innovation and conflict and do so to a greater degree as the social structure becomes weaker.

Richard Cloward amplifies this position in an important study of a military prison, to which reference has already been made.[35] The setting was a barracks-type institution housing 1,500 inmates under medium security conditions. The men were confined for sentences ranging from six months to life for violations of military law, and all had been dishonorably discharged from the military forces.

Upon intake the men received the usual exhortations to good conduct. In addition, they were promised that if an inmate scrupulously avoided getting involved with other men and maintained a good conduct record in the institution, he had an excellent chance to be restored to military duty and eventually to receive an honorable discharge. As one prisoner explained, "The colonel said our chances was 50-50. I think I have a good chance to go back if I don't mess up, and right now I don't intend to mess up." At the beginning of institutionalization, restoration was sought by 70 percent of the inmates. Six months later restoration was sought by only 45 percent of the men. At least 30 percent of the men had adopted the role of passive non-cooperation. They became involved in the informal, illegitimate social system of the prison and exhibited various forms of misconduct -- smuggling, possessing contraband, hostility toward officers -- in short, all that they had been warned against.

-7-

An important feature of Cloward's study is that the misbehavior of the military inmates cannot be explained by the process of socialization into a "criminal culture." Men are discharged from military service for the kinds of crimes these men committed; hence they must have all been first offenders. Presumably, a criminal sub-world does not exist in the armed forces. The very high percentage of men who first believed the promises offered by the system, and applied for restoration, is further evidence that the typical offender was one who had accepted his guilt and aspired to a legitimate role. How is the frequent abandonment of this aspiration to be explained?

Cloward's analysis is quite simple. The men, he says, came to doubt that restoration was a realistic goal for them. Their fellow inmates told them of the small proportion of men who achieved restoration and of the prejudice against certain types of offense categories. Once they become convinced of the validity of the new information, they lack a rational motivation for conformity. In Merton's terms, the inmates lacked opportunity for the achievement of the culturally prescribed goals. The military prison is one of those social systems which has induced its members to want that which cannot be obtained. Its own defeat quickly follows.

The previously mentioned study of Oahu Prison by McCleery makes use of a basically rational perspective in explaining prison conflict, albeit a sophisticated and elegant conception of how rational divergencies come into being. In this prison a custody-oriented warden had held sway. Under this condition, "a few aging and ill-educated custodians, as few as eight men to a night watch, could control 400 bitter and frustrated fellows...."[36] As we earlier pointed out, McCleery attributes this unusual control to the support of the ideal of peace and order by inmate leaders. The leaders gained support from their followers by disbursing to their underlings the privileges they had gained from the staff, while at the same time paying lip service to the cultural ideal of antagonism toward the staff. The tenuous nature of the support for the norm that prescribed stability is examined in McCleery's study.

In 1946 the prison began a long process of reorganization under a modern administration. The new administration removed all the privileges that custodial officers had been handing out to the old inmate leaders. This reduced the incentive of the leaders to maintain peace, and furthermore reduced their ability to reward their followers with privilege handouts (such as access to illegal alcohol, good jobs, etc.). Within a few years, major infractions of prison rules reached a level 400 percent above the period prior to 1946.[37] While it was not the old inmate leaders who led the conflict, they remained passive while new leaders, oriented toward extremes of violence, took their place. In short, the staff can buy reduction of conflict with tenders of privilege. Elimination of such informal privilege creates conflict. However, another point emerges.

Under the new administrative policy, privileges were offered by the treatment staff for behavior in accord with treatment goals. Such offerings did not produce good behavior, in contrast to the old arrangements. Under the old system, inmates made the exchange of good behavior for privilege with inmate leaders, and inmate leaders made the same exchange with custodial officers. Such behavior strongly smacks of the soldier who will not make his personal peace with the enemy but is quite delighted when his leaders do so. Why rationality takes this peculiar form is an important question for theory to answer.

Another study that serves as a typical example of the rational view of conflict is the well-known "Robber's Cave" research by Sherif and associates.[38] Sherif rejected the traditional notion that face-to-face contact between members of warring groups will tend to reduce conflict. He found that contact served only to increase the number of unpleasant incidents. Sherif proposed two hypotheses about the reduction of conflict and offered evidence regarding the behavior of two groups of boys who had experienced intergroup conflict in a summer camp.

1. When groups in a boys camp are brought into contact under conditions embodying superordinate goals, the attainment of which is impelling but which cannot be achieved by the efforts of one group alone, they will tend to cooperate towards a common goal.

Such cooperation on specifics did not immediately change the relationship between the groups, once the superordinate goals had been achieved.

2. Cooperation between groups necessitated by a series of such situations embodying superordinate goals will have a cumulative effect in the direction of reduction of existing tensions between groups.[39]

Superordinate goals, as retional reasons for the reduction of conflict, appear to be different than promises of privilege by the prison staff. In the latter situation each group has a different goal; the staff wishes to reduce misconduct and the inmate wishes to obtain privileges. As we have seen, such a situation often fails to achieve reduction of conflict. Sometimes superordinate goals come to exist in the inmate-staff relationship.

...Inmates have been employed against the hazards of flood and forest fire. The heroism of inmates in such crises has moved some commentators to assert that convicts are quite like other people, when, in fact, other people were probably retreating in panic.[40]

Such dramatic evidence of change of behavior is not to be taken as fleeting expressions of humanitarianism by basically incorrigible individuals. The goal of fighting fire or flood is different than the goal of getting into the mess hall on time. The latter is of no intrinsic importance to the inmates, while the former is. Inmates have told the author that they enjoy fighting fire because they get good food, get paid, and get treated like civilians. The observer could not help but feel that there was something special about this experience that went beyond their prosaic explanations, even though it appeared to be necessary for them to offer selfish rather than social explanations of their good conduct.

Sherif does not recognize that there is something different about superordinate goals as compared to other rational motives for conduct and does not inquire into the theoretical reasons why superordinate goals should have the effect that they do have. Apparently, he feels that his propositions are self-explanatory. We shall inquire into these issues again, later in the discussion.

In summary, the rational approach states that conflict will occur when rational interests make conflict useful; it will diminish when rational interests make cooperation useful. We have seen the dual perspective that rationality may be promoted by conditions of moral disintegration, and also that rational motivations may promote the process of moral disintegration (Merton). It has been noted that group processes make only certain kinds of rational exchanges possible (McCleery), and we suggested an interpretation of the Sherif finding that <u>common</u> rational goals reduce conflict.

The Functional School of Conflict

A third approach is exemplified in the work of Closer, who examines a series of propositions drawn from Simmel's work on conflict.[41] He calls attention to the many consequences of conflict for creating functional properties of groups. "Conflict unites unrelated persons." The functions of conflict for the attainment of high morale were also noted by Sherif in the Robber's Cave study.[42] The functional consequences of conflict give it certain social rationality, even if it leads to some undesirable consequences as well.

The functionalist view, but itself, offers us no very clear explanation of why the world is not split up into continually warring camps, since all conflict is apparently equally functional for all groups. It is, of course, possible to disagree with the latter assertion and argue that conflict is most useful for groups that do not have a good basis for internal cohesion and "need" an external enemy to bind the members. Workers in correctional institutions will testify to the negative feelings inmates have about their fellow inmates. By heightening hostility toward the staff, conflict may serve to de-emphasize these negative feelings.

The rational and functionalist points of view may be combined. It then becomes possible to answer the question of why the world is not continually at war by asserting that when rational motives for cooperation are not present conflict will invariably occur. Conflict, it can be argued, is the natural state of things since it is not only useful but "fun"[43] as well. However, rational motives for cooperation are often present, and so groups either pick only certain targets for antagonism or subside into an uneasy state of peace.

The functional school also leaves unanswered the problem of why a group should choose an outside group as its target rather than carry on internecine wars. The functional view is a kind of single insight which has a predictive value only when combined with other propositions about group process. After conflict occurs, it can be given a functional explanation by reference to the consequences of the behavior. But most important, the functional approach offers us little understanding of the way in which the functional consequences of conflict <u>become converted into the motives of the actors we are studying</u>.

Process Approaches to Conflict

Nonetheless, all of them focus on some single facet, and all fail to give consideration to the <u>process</u> by which conflict behavior results from the conjunction of individual motivations and a structural context (both group and interpersonal), both of which dispose toward conflict. Sayles, in his work on industrial conflict, takes a preliminary step in this direction.[44] He considers the kinds of deprivations suffered by workers, but also takes into account their ability to communicate and thus collectivize their grievances. The latter depends on the facility for communication of feelings that exists in group settings in which they experience the deprivation. Sayles offers a number of findings about the types of groups which have the tendency to rapidly communicate grievances. Lipset approaches the study of extremist voting in a similar fashion.[45] Cohen goes beyond Merton both in pointing out the social psychological _meaning_ of status deprivation for the self image and also in asking how the social structure affects the individual's tendency to cope with this problem by means of conflict behavior.[46] Similar questions are asked by Cloward and Ohlin.[47]

We shall attempt to further integrate the various theoretical formulations so as to be able to offer some original propositions on conflict behavior and to suggest ways in which the propositions may be tested in a correctional setting. The importance of attempting an integration of the various approaches is twofold. First, the integration may uncover basic consistencies and inconsistencies in the various approches. Thus, crucial issues may develop which will require resolution. The consistencies in the models may suggest new ways in which quite general hypotheses can be formulated. Second, this author feels that the character of conflict behavior requires that its development be conceived as a process and that many occurrences in the life of individuals or groups must coalesce to predispose them toward conflict. The absence of certain links, it is felt, will change the entire nature of the eventual behavior.

There is considerable evidence that when conflict occurs it has a far more total effect on group life than do other group characteristics. What we normally think of as conflict is more analogous to group _goal_ than to those commonplace standards we think of as _norms_. Norms are prescriptions for behavior under special and limited circumstances. Conflict, on the other hand, dominates the life of the group and compels every member to subordinate all his other interests to the general effort.

Now, if the preceding assertions are correct, it seems likely that individual propositions of the kind "if A then B" may hold under only rather specific conditions. The confusing evidence about the different kinds of rational motivations that will or will not produce conflict or cooperation seems evidence in point. Integration of the various viewpoints may provide an understanding of the specific conditions under which the individual propositions about conflict are true or false.

FOOTNOTES

[1] Both Dahrendorf and Coser make this point with much cogency. Ralf Dahrendorf, "Out of Utopia: Toward a Reorientation of Sociological Analysis," _American Journal of Sociology_, LXIV (September, 1958), 128-136; Lewis A. Coser, _The Functions of Social Conflict_ (Glencoe, Ill.: The Free Press, 1956), Introduction, pp. 15-31. Coser suggests that conflict as a phenomenon was of greater importance earlier in the history of sociology. On the other hand, Dahrendorf feels that a conflict model of society is beginning to gain ground in sociological analysis.

[2] Two modern representatives of the economist's interest in conflict are Boulding and Schelling. Kenneth E. Boulding, *Conflict and Defense* (New York: Harper and Brothers, 1962); Thomas C. Schelling, *The Strategy of Conflict* (Cambridge, Mass.: Harvard University Press, 1960). Marx was an early student of conflict, of course. As an economist, he sought to trace out the consequences of marketplace arrangements for the development of objective divergencies of interest. As a sociologist, he sought to explain the rise of class consciousness and the consequent development of overt conflict. See the analysis of Marx in Ralf Dahrendorf, *Class and Class Conflict in an Industrial Society* (Stanford; Stanford University Press, 1959), Part I. Also see J.A. Schumpeter, *Capitalism, Socialism and Democracy* (New York: Harper and Brothers, 1950).

[3] There are exceptions to the above statement. European sociologists, especially Simmel, displayed a strong interest in conflict. See Don Martindale, *The Nature and Types of Sociological Theory* (Cambridge, Mass.: The Riverside Press, 1960), Part III; Georg Simmel, *Conflict and the Web of Group Affiliation* (Glencoe, Ill.: The Free Press, 1955). Conflict was an important concept in the ecological work of Park and Burgess. It is of interest that Park and Burgess utilized a definition of ecology that had a strongly economic basis. Robert E. Park and Ernest W. Burgess, *Introduction to the Science of Sociology* (Chicago: University of Chicago Press, 1921; 2nd ed., 1924); Robert E. Park, "Human Ecology," *American Journal of Sociology*, XLII (July, 1936), 1-15. "Society, as ecologists have conceived it, is a population settled and limited to its habitat. The ties that unite its natural units are those of a free and natural economy, based on a natural division of labor . . . . The ties which hold it together are physical and vital rather than customary and moral." (p. 15)

[4] James S. Coleman, *Community Conflict* (Glencoe, Ill.: The Free Press, 1957); Hadley Cantril, *The Politics of Despair* (New York: Basic Books, 1958); Seymour M. Lipset, *Political Man* (New York: Doubleday, 1959); Leonard Sayles, *Behavior of Industrial Work Groups* (New York: Wiley, 1958); Richard H. McCleery, "The Governmental Process and Informal Social Control" and "Authoritarianism and the Belief System of Incorrigibles" in Donald R. Cressey (ed.), *The Prison* (New York: Holt, Rinehart, and Winston, 1961), pp. 149-188, 260-306.

[5] Stanton Wheeler, "Social Organization in a Correctional Community" (unpublished Ph.D. dissertation, University of Washington, Seattle, 1958); Richard Cloward, discussant in Helen Leland Witmer and Ruth Kotinsky (eds.), *New Perspectives for Research on Juvenile Delinquency* (Washington, D.C.: United States Department of Health, Education, and Welfare, Children's Bureau Publication No. 356, 1956), pp. 80-91.

[6] Samuel A. Stouffer, et al., *The American Soldier*, Vol. I (Princeton, N.J.: Princeton University Press, 1949), pp. 368-375. Note also the second and fourth tables on page 417. According to these tables, 72 percent of enlisted men thought that it was wrong to break army regulations, even if they wouldn't get caught; yet only 19 percent of the enlisted men agreed that most enlisted men obeyed the rules, not because they wanted to, but because they had to. This suggests a pattern of pluralistic ignorance.

[7] Donald Clemmer, The Prison Community (New York: Rinehart and Co., 1958), p. 299.

[8] Ibid., p. 302.

[9] Donald R. Cressey, "Limitations on Organization of Treatment in the Modern Prison" in Theoretical Studies in the Social Organization of the Prison (New York: Social Science Research Council, Pamphlet No. 15), pp. 78-110.

[10] Ralf Dahrendorf, "Out of Utopia: Toward a Reorientation of Sociological Analysis," American Journal of Sociology, LXIV (September, 1958), 120.

[11] See his discussion of effectiveness, which can keep illegitimate governments in power. Seymour M. Lipset, "Political Sociology" in Robert K. Merton, Leonard Broom, and Leonard S. Cottrell (eds.), Sociology Today (New York: Basic Books, 1959), pp. 108-110.

[12] For example, Hans J. Morgenthau, Politics among Nations (New York: Alfred A. Knopf, 1948).

[13] Elton Mayo, The Social Problems of an Industrial Civilization (Boston: Harvard University Press, 1945). According to Mayo, "economist's presuppositions of individual self-preservation" conflict with "the desire to stand well with one's fellows . . . ." (p. 42). According to Mayo (p. 42) and to Roethlisberger and Dickson, the desire to stand well with one's fellows is responsible for work restriction. F.J. Roethlisberger and William J. Dickson, Management and the Worker (Cambridge, Mass.: Harvard University Press, 1939), Part IV.

[14] Frederic M. Thrasher, The Gang (Chicago: The University of Chicago Press, 1927). Thrasher does point to the difference between "solidified" gangs, with a well-developed tradition, and "diffuse" gangs, which exert few effective pressures on their members. See Chapter IV.

[15] Edwin H. Sutherland, Principles of Criminology (fourth edition) Philadelphia: J.B. Lippincott Co., 1947, Chapter I.

[16] Walter B. Miller, "Lower Class Culture as a Generating Milieu of Gang Delinquency," Journal of Social Issues, XIV:3 (1958), 5-19.

[17] Wheeler, op. cit.

[18] Wheeler, op. cit., pp. 88-91.

[19] Peter G. Garabedian, "Western Penitentiary: A Study in Social Organization" (unpublished Ph.D. dissertation, University of Washington, Seattle, 1959), pp. 78-80.

[20] Richard H. McCleery, "The Governmental Process and Informal Social Control" in Donald R. Cressey (ed.), The Prison (New York: Holt, Rinehart and

Winston, 1961), pp. 149-188; Richard Cloward, "Social Control in the Prison," in Theoretical Studies in the Social Organization of the Prison (New York: Social Science Research Council, Pamphlet No. 15, 1960), pp. 45-48.

[21] Cloward, ibid., p. 47 (Italics provided).

[22] Roethlisberger and Dickson, op. cit., p. 522; Stouffer, et al., op. cit., pp. 420-421.

[23] McCleery, op. cit., pp. 149-188.

[24] For a more elaborate description of the informal exchanges, see Gresham M. Sykes, "The Corruption of Authority and Rehabilitation," Social Forces, XXXIV (March, 1956), 257-262.

[25] McCleery, op. cit., p. 164.

[26] Stanton Wheeler, "Role Conflict in Correctional Communities" in Donald R. Cressey (ed.), The Prison (New York: Holt, Rinehart, and Winston, 1961), pp. 249-255.

[27] Quoted in Ralf Dahrendorf, Class and Class Conflict in an Industrial Society (Stanford: Stanford University Press, 1959), p. 14.

[28] Ibid., p. 13.

[29] George Vold, Theoretical Criminology (New York: Oxford University Press, 1958), pp. 208-209.

[30] Robert K. Merton, "Social Structure and Anomie," American Sociological Review, III (October, 1938), 672-682.

[31] Richard A. Cloward, "Illegitimate Means, Anomie, and Deviant Behavior," American Sociological Review, XXIV (April, 1959), 164-176.

[32] Albert K. Cohen, Delinquent Boys (Glencoe, Ill.: The Free Press, 1955).

[33] Merton, op. cit.

[34] Ibid., p. 682.

[35] Richard Cloward, New Perspectives for Research on Juvenile Delinquency (Washington, D.C.: Children's Bureau Publication No. 356, 1956), pp. 80-91.

[36] Richard H. McCleery, "Communications Patterns as a Basis of Systems of Authority and Power" in Theoretical Studies in the Social Organization of the Prison (New York: Social Science Research Council Pamphlet No. 15, 1960), p. 56.

[37] McCleery, op. cit., p. 179.

[38] Muzafer Sherif, et al., <u>Intergroup Conflict and Cooperation: The Robber's Cave Experiment</u> (Norman, Oklahoma: Institute of Group Relations, University of Oklahoma, 1961).

[39] Ibid., p. 52.

[40] McCleery, op. cit., p. 181.

[41] Lewis A. Coser, <u>The Functions of Social Conflict</u> (Glencoe, Ill.: The Free Press, 1956), p. 121.

[42] Sherif, et al., op. cit., pp. 117-126. Sherif notes that each group experienced internal friction following a defeat at the hands of the other group, but that solidarity was retrieved and even heightened by behaving in an aggressive fashion toward the "enemy" group of boys.

[43] Correctional workers sometimes attribute prison riots to the desire of inmates to reliev the boredom of life inside the walls, especially in summertime when the inmates are aware of all the fun they are missing.

[44] Leonard R. Sayles, <u>Behavior of Industrial Work Groups</u> (New York: Wiley, 1958).

[45] Seymour Martin Lipset, <u>Political Man</u> (New York: Doubleday, 1959), especially Chapters 6, 7, and 8.

[46] Albert K. Cohen, <u>Delinquent Boys</u> (Glencoe, Ill.: The Free Press, 1955).

[47] Richard A. Cloward and Lloyd E. Ohlin, <u>Delinquency and Opportunity</u> (Glencoe, Ill.: The Free Press, 1960).

CHAPTER II

A SOCIAL-PSYCHOLOGICAL THEORY OF CONFLICT

A DEFINITION

So far in the present study no definition of the term "conflict" has been offered. This has been deliberate, because the various approaches reviewed use somewhat different definitions. A definition must be offered, however. Let us examine four alternatives:

1. Conflict refers to the existence of strong differences of opinion about what ought to be done in any specific situation.

2. Conflict refers to the differing behaviors which result from the strong differences of opinion referred to above.

3. Conflict refers to "all relations between sets of individuals that involve an incompatible difference of objective, i.e., in its most general form, a desire on the part of both contestants to attain what is available to one, or only in part, (being) in this sense, relations of social conflict." [1]

4. Conflict refers to "a situation of competition in which the parties are aware of the incompatibility of potential future positions and in which each party wishes to occupy a position that is incompatible with the wishes of the other." [2]

The first definition -- conflict, in opinions, about possible actions -- is a common way in which the term is used. A husband and wife who are contemplating a night of entertainment may disagree about which movie is most perferable. This definition equates conflict with dissensus and is the sense in which Wheeler used the term "role conflict" in his description of inmate-staff disagreements. Such disagreements, of course, *may* stem from different role prescriptions. Disagreement, however, occurs more or less continuously in human life, but generally results in some sort of working agreement about what behaviors to follow. Even rather large differences are amicably resolved in the typical case. If conflict is defined as dissensus, even <u>persistent</u> dissensus, conflict becomes the usual pattern, rather than an unusual interaction state.

The second definition refers to differences of behavior. In a special way it differs from the first definition, because behavoir has certain consequences for the future that attitudinal disagreement is less likely to have. A husband and wife who disagree may decide to go to separate movies. A number of consequences might follow. In the first place, both parties may be hurt that their mate did not make the sacrifice for them. It can even be argued that a person does not know if he is truly loved unless the other party does something he does not wish to do, for that love. (It can be further argued, therefore, that dissensus is necessary as confirmation of a smooth-working, affectionate human relation.) The parties going their separate ways may feel that a decline in the affectional character of their marriage has occurred. Furthermore, the spouses may discover that it is oossible to enjoy a movie alone. Thus, a new state may begin between the parties. Had they compromised on a single choice, had they behaved identically, the new state would not have occurred. Of course, the spouses may find the experience quite unpleasant and may return to one another with apologies and demonstrations of affection. These important symbolic acts occur because of the realization that insistence on separate behaviors has pushed them toward a new state which they do not wish to accept. Behavior forms an important part of our definition.

The third definition, used by Dahrendorf in his study of class conflict, differs from the first in that it refers to a difference of objective, rather than to a simple disagreement. Simple differences often do not need to be resolved; the parties may pursue their courses independently. Differences of objective are more likely to need resolution, and incompatible differences almost require resolution for action to take place. Dahrendorf's conflict thus creates more of a problem for the parties than does a simple conflict of preferences. Dahrenforf was interested in pursuing the notion that conflict is normal and pervasive in a group. His conflict certainly is quite common and is usually resolved by some sort of compromise. Compromise is possible because each individual has a series of objectives and is willing to sacrifice one of them to achieve others. Incidentally, Dahrendorf's definition has occassionally been used as a hypothesis about conflict; it has been argued that conflict occurs when each party desires a course of action that is incompatible with the values sought by the other party. We shall refer to this hypothesis later. An important feature of this third definition is that it does not clearly refer to behavior.

In the fourth definition, Boulding offers something new with the idea that the parties are aware of the incompatibility. It may be that most conflicts in Dahrendorf's sense are resolved at the stage at which the parties become aware of the differences. They did not mean to be in conflict and have a desire to attenuate any conflict that occurs. Boulding's parties mean to be in conflict. They want to occupy an incompatible position. Boulding comes closer than do the others to describing an affective state between individuals or groups. But, like Dahrendorf, Boulding is not referring to behavior but to attitudes. To go back to the marital situation, it is doubtless common for one spouse to desire things he well knows are incompatible with the wishes of the other. As we have pointed out, people are typically limited in the willingness to convert wishes into actions because behavior may be far more disruptive to interpersonal relations than are wishes. Dahrendorf defined conflict as relationships that involve incompatible objectives. We would argue that it is very difficult to know, in advance, what such relationships might be like. It is interesting to contrast his definition to that formulated earlier by Park and Burgess. What Dahrendorf calls conflict, Park and Burgess called competition. Competition was viewed as the pre-social struggle for survival; it initiates conflict, accommodation, and assimilation. Conflict is competition lifted to a conscious and social level. "Conflict is to be identified with the political order and conscious control." [3]

There is not arguing about the validity of definitions. One can merely point to the differences in their referents and decide which referents are the most appropriate for one's own interests. The preference for the referent "group state" has already been suggested. Actually, this is a referent that is very common in the use of the term conflict to describe wars, minority tensions, prison riots, and similar phenomena. Let us offer our own definition.

Conflict refers to a state having the following four elements:

1. The parties have preference for a variety of behaviors that are incompatible with salient wishes of the other party. These preferences have (a) some degree of generality and (b) some degree of importance to the other.

2. The parties are aware of the incompatibility of their preferences with the wishes of the other. Party A knows that his preferences are disliked by Party B, and the incompatibilities form an important part of his conception of his relation to Party B. The incompatible wishes need not be total and probably never are, but the parties conceive of them as relatively total.

3. The preferences are expressed in behavior.

4. The parties have an organizational tie to one another. Conflict is <u>interaction</u>, not the acts of one individual, that produces no response from the other. Americans do not come into conflict with the Andamanese, even though many differences in behavior exist. Even if aware of these differences, they rarely create discomfort.

Let us go back to the prison situation. The fact that there are differences in the norms of inmates and staff should not lead us to characterize the situations as conflict. However, if we find that the norms involved tend to be polar opposites, we may suspect that the normative differences are the product of a consistent tendency to positively value that which the other party dislikes. Normative differences can be viewed as a <u>consequence</u> of conflict, as well as a cause of it. Normative differences, however, usually refer to attitudes and we wish to emphasize behavior. Do the parties make the minor adjustments necessary to soften the effect of differences? Both Cloward and McCleery suggest that this is the usual case. The inmate leaders, or the inmate culture, advise some degree of moderation. "Engage in smuggling, collect contraband, but don't assault a guard, don't refuse to work, don't smash your toilet in anger." As Cloward puts it, the role of passive non-cooperation is prescribed, not total war.[4] Sherif's boys seem to have approached closer to a full blown state of conflict. They found a wide variety of ways of offending one another -- shoving in line, dirty epithets, nasty signs, raids, etc. -- <u>although their respective group norms were quite similar.</u>[5]

SOME BASIC TERMS

<u>Threat</u>: A state in which there is a marked reduction in the ability of an organism to maintain an attribute that it is strongly motivated to maintain. A <u>perceived threat</u> is a threat that has been recognized by the party or parties involved.

<u>Dominance relations</u>: Interaction whose primary effect is to establish an answer to the question, "Who is controlling the behavior of the parties to the interaction?"

<u>Balanced exchange relationship</u>: An interaction in which the social value of that which is given is equal to the social value of that which is received.

<u>Real threat</u>: A threat which affects only an individual's publicly defined character, not his private view of himself.

<u>Psychological threat</u>: A threat which affects an individual's private view of himself. A threat may be psychological but not real, if it is only perceived by the party to whom it applies.

<u>Perceived source of demands</u>: The inference a person makes as to whether his behavior is a response to (1) his own wishes, or (2) the wishes of some specific other or others, or (3) a rational response to a situation which has no clear reference to any specific other or others.

<u>Status</u>: The position of an individual in some specific social hierarchy.

<u>Identification</u>: An affective and cognitive relationship between two or more parties which is characterized by feelings of <u>similarity</u> and <u>attraction</u>.

<u>Negotiated reward</u>: A type of reward which is given only temporarily, for the short run; the reward is the subject of continual bargaining. Negotiated reward is characteristic of experiments with laboratory animals. Human beings normally acquire a <u>right</u> to certain rewards, which can be lost only by long-run failure to meet the <u>obligations</u> that are associated with the reward. A grade on a weekly or mid-term examination is a negotiated reward; once the final course grade is received, it is a right.

SOME BASIC PROPOSITIONS

Dominance and Conflict

Let us begin with one elementary proposition.

1. When various parties are involved in a state of conflict, their interaction will be evaluated by the parties primarily in terms of its meaning for the relative dominance of the respective parties.

This proposition states that the primary symbolic dimension for conflicting parties will be that of dominance. A nice illustration of this kind of behavior is given by Scudder in his description of the treatment of striking prisoners at San Quentin:

> In front of each cell in the large corridor, a solid white circle, 22 inches in diameter, was painted on the floor. Each day the men were taken from their cells and ordered to stand at attention and remain there seven and eight hours, except for two rest periods of five minutes each to go to the toilet. If any man moved or spoke, he was subject to a severe beating.
>
> The lieutenant entered and held a hurried whispered conversation with the guards. Then in a raucous tone he bellowed, "You bastards will get six months in solitary for starting this food riot."
>
> Like an electric shock his words seemed to pass from body to body. Six months in solitary also meant six months on the spot. -- They glanced hopelessly about. Some dropped to the floor exhausted, unable to rise. Pandemonium broke loose; guards shouted at the men to get up. Some clambered to their feet; others refused and sat sprawled on the cold cement floor. Then, slowly, one by one, the seated men arose to resume their positions of attention.
>
> The lieutenant was like a madman as he paraded up and down the corridor, glowering at the men. "You birds want trouble," he said, "I'm going to give you plenty."[6]

Scudder goes on to an account of a brutal beating, delivered indiscriminately to all the prisoners except one, who, because he had a double hernia, was given the special treatment of a beating on his swollen groins. The prison board supported the beatings on the grounds that the guards had used their best judgment in quelling a near riot.

What had the inmates done to provoke the response of the guards? If one argues that conflict refers to large discrepancies in behavior relative to the demands of the parties, the behavior of the inmates is hardly an example of conflict on their part. They merely moved a few inches, or were temporarily unable or unwilling to behave in the exact way the guards demanded. But they all resumed standing on the spot.

What the guards responded to, it would seem, was not the negligible difference between inmate behavior and the guards' expectations, but the symbolic difference. The inmates were those who were perceived as most defiant toward staff authority. All the inmates had gone on strike, but these particular inmates were thought to be the leaders. The staff was trying to show who had the ultimate authority, and said, in effect, we can make you stand exactly on the spot for six months. Once having made this kind of implicit statement about staff power, any deviation from their demands would have been a demonstration that the staff was weak. If the staff had said, "You stay within six feet of the spot," then moving off the spot would not have been a threat to their authority. The staff set its own terms for the conflict, once it stated its wishes. When conflict has reached the extreme level we see here, the dominance-submission perspective becomes so all-important that any deviation from command, even those due to the effects of heat, exhaustion, and psychological withdrawal, are perceived as attacks on the guards' authority.

From the inmates's perspective, the same process may be occurring. The inmate wishes to express his own resistance. He does this, not by total defiance; he need only move a few inches off the spot to say, "You're not the boss." The staff has clearly indicated the precise manner in which it may be defied. Probably the inmates refrained from total defiance because they feared the massacre it might provoke, though in this sense the guards' response was underestimated.

Scudder tells us that an officer stood by during the beatings ready to shoot any inmate who attacked his tormentor. The guards were aware of the extent to which they were provoking the inmates.

Coleman points out that the observer who arrives on the scene when a conflict is in feverish heat is like a sober man arriving at a drunken party.[7] Where others laugh at silly jokes, he is disgusted. But the jokes really are funny to the participants, and in the conflict situation we may add that the "reasonable man" may be quite wrong in his perception of the social realities. It may well be true that when the inmate steps off the spot he means to attack the authority of the guard -- because both he and the guard have agreed on the symbolic meaning of events. Coser presents further examples of symbols of dominance in conflict.[8] Party A may announce, "We will defend Jonesville to the last man." Having done this, the parties, in effect, may come to agree that this city is the supreme symbol of dominance. If Jonesville is subsequently lost, Party A is more than likely to capitulate. The parties become so completely absorbed in this symbol of dominance that they are unable to recognise that Party A may not yet be completely helpless (from the point of view of the reasonable man). In some sense Party A is helpless, since the loss of the city has given an immeasurable boost to the morale of the enemy and demoralized its own forces. The fall of the city has shown them, perhaps inaccurately, the great power of the enemy. A call to arms will not suffice, without redefining the symbols of dominance.

Our second proposition is partly drawn from the first.

2. Conflict tends to be a mutually reinforcing relationship.

This proposition states that the level of conflict does not vary randomly but tends to be stable or to continue in the direction in which it is already moving. Coleman has pointed out that conflict -- or its opposite, cooperation -- tends to have a mutually reinforcing character. This is probably the most important single characteristic of conflict behavior. In the San Quentin situation, the behavior of the staff had the forseeable consequence of making the inmates more rebellious. But the inmates' rebellious behavior had the consequence of provoking even more hostile responses from the guards. Thus a seemingly never-ending cycle of attack and counter-attack develops. <u>In a situation in which the parties are oriented in terms of dominance-submission, we hypothesize that the normal response to attack is to do things that promote further attack.</u> This assertion is not to be taken as a reference to unknown or unconscious processes. Often the parties are aware, even in the irrationality of extreme conflict, of the provocative character of their behavior. Yet they find it necessary to make the symbolic gesture of dominance. One cannot help inferring that the "madman-like" behavior of the lieutenant was partly a function of fear. How would the inmates respond? They might defy the lieutenant's authority (which is becoming increasingly open to question -- the angrier he gets, the more any slight deviation becomes a severe attack); they might try to kill him. In short, the initiation of conflict tends to set in motion a train of forces that maintain the conflict, regardless of the forces which began the process.

Two corollaries to the second proposition are: (1) for conflict to continue, both parties must accept the same definition of the symbols of dominance; and (2) only if both parties evaluate interaction in the terms of relative dominance can conflict continue or be initiated. Both these corollaries argue that all sides must "assent" to the conflict. If the inmates attach different significance to the symbols than does the staff, conflict will be dissipated. Bettleheim states that politically oriented prisoners "found support for their self-esteem in the fact that the Gestapo had singled them out as important enough to take revenge on."[9] Instead of symbolizing the dominance of the staff, mistreatment symbolizes the dominance of the prisoner. In consequence, we would argue, politically oriented prisons were able to avoid the ravaging warfare of open conflict and instead engaged in quiet underground activities.[10] While conflict did not cease, it diminished considerably.

The second corollary is closely related to the first because, if one does not evaluate interaction in terms of the dominance dimension, obviously the symbols of dominance are meaningless. Redl and Wineman give a fine example of how one can avoid conflict by applying corollary two.[11] In Pioneer House they were faced with the problem of how to handle aggressive children. Attempts at normal discipline would provoke even more aggressive behavior from the children. A set of simple devices was invoked. The first rule was that one must not deal with aggression by showing <u>anger</u>. Second, if the child became too aggressive, he was "bounced" -- taken out of the group without the use of brute force. Third, the therapist was to stay with the child and help deal with the feelings that were generated. All these mechanisms showed the child that the therapist did not accept the behavior as an attack on himself. He would neither respond to the behavior provocatively <u>nor indicate that his lack of a provocative response</u> indicated submission. Unlike the San Quentin staff member, he did not put his authority to a test by saying, in effect, "If you can stand off the spot, you have destroyed my authority." There is nothing the child can do to win, but he is not losing, either.

One difficulty with Redl and Wineman's approach is that it is not easy to respond in non-dominance terms to a consistently aggressive party. The other party does not initially respond to one's non-dominant behavior in one's own terms, but instead acts as if he has won the battle. Redl and Wineman describe an afternoon which had been especially positive after the "very happy special treat of horseback riding." One of the children -- Joe -- says to the counselor (who was no doubt feeling successful at this point),

> very softly, slightly mimicking her soft Canadian accent, "Vera?" "Yes, Joe?" To which he replied just as softly, "Are you gonna take a shit when we get home?" The group responded by cackles and snorts of derision.[12]

It seems quite difficult to avoid responding by anger and validating the child's conception that he is doing battle with the staff member. Alternatively, to become embarrassed validates the child's conceptual system and tells him that he is victorious, at least temporarily. Corollary two stated that both parties must view the interaction in dominance terms, for conflict to be initiated. It should be added that it is normally sufficient for only one party to view the interaction in dominance terms, because he is likely to provoke the other person into holding an identical view, thus beginning the cycle of mutual reinforcement of conflict behavior.

Thus, our third proposition states:

3. If any of the parties to an interaction evaluate the interaction in terms of its effects on dominance relations, conflict is likely to occur.

One further point is in order and creates a major exception to proposition two. One of the possible results of conflict is defeat of one of the parties. This is the result both inmate and staff were hoping for at San Quentin. When the parties come to agree on some major symbol of dominance and one is able to successfully demonstrate its dominance by means of this symbol, it may achieve the sudden and total collapse of the other. Total defeat does not happen very often in human interaction, but it may happen more often to individuals who are strongly focused on the dominance dimension. The California Authoritarian Personality" research lends some support to this notion. It was found that those subjects who were highly concerned with symbols of authority tended to include polar opposites -- subjects who were oriented toward dominance and subjects oriented toward submission.[13] Thus inmates who are strongly conflict oriented, especially those who have "major symbols," sometimes feel defeated and become submissive where out-siders find no great reason for their discomfiture. The conditions which produce this submission are yet to be described, and therefore we should say that "conflict is a mutually reinforced state, except that it occassionally may produce unpredictable and dramatic changes." It is important to reduce this unpredictability.

Dominance and Threat

A fourth proposition refers to the kinds of situations that tend to produce movement onto the dominance dimension.

4. Strong threats to the self-esteem, especially in terms of conception of self as autonomous and powerful, will tend to produce movement onto the dominance dimension.

Bettleheim's work on the concentration camp is a classic description of proposition four. The inmates were subjected to brutal treatment by the guards, and moreover treatment which seems designed to "strip" the inmate of former statuses and to debase him.

> These tortures alternated with efforts on the part of guards to force the prisoners to hurt one another and to defile what the guards considered the prisoner's most cherished values. For instance, the prisoners were forced to curse their God, to accuse themselves of vile actions, accuse their wives of adultery and prostitution.[14]

For the prisoners, the major life problem was to continue to believe that they were important, respectible persons, notwithstanding all the negative evidence they were getting in this regard. By and large, the threat did not produce conflict behavior -- the prisoners were well aware of the terrible revenge that the guards would inflict on any signs of rebellion. Instead, a common reaction is to develop a feeling of detachment that says, in effect, "this is happening to my body, not to my self." Thus the inmate avoids the threat to self temporarily. Ultimately, however, the inmate emulates the tough, brutal behavior of the guards, demonstrating his personal power not by attacking the powerful Gestapo but by exerting dominance over other persons.

In order to show why it was that the inmates did not come into conflict with the guards, a distinction should be drawn between psychological threat to the self-esteem and "real threat." Psychological threat is the sort of experience that destroys the inmate's conception of his ability to be a powerful person; it attacks his very foundation. This kind of attack may occur to students as a result of poor grades on examinations. On the other hand, a "real threat" refers to an aggressive attack on oneself by another which is a threat to one's publicly presented self rather tna to one's private self image. When a guard, who has all the tools of power at his disposal, beats up an inmate or forces him to do an unpleasant job, he does not thereby prove the inmate to be a weakling. To put this in our own language, the attack becomes a symbol of dominance. A counterattack reasserts the inmate's intention to retain his relative dominance. A psychological threat has occurred where, due to some major failure to make an effective counterattack or due to his unwillingness to counterattack at all, the inmate feels he has lost his ability to be powerful. Psychological threat may produce submission (a partial answer to the question of proposition three) or a conflict relation that is ororiented toward all people, rather than toward the aggressor alone. Real threat is likely to produce a counterattack toward the specific aggressor. The peculiar response of the concentration camp inmates in becoming aggressive toward other inmates may have been due to the psychological threat they experienced.

The present discussion of real and psychological threat parallels that of Cloward and Ohlin, to some degree. They point out that some people who fail blame themselves for the failure; others blame the system.[15] In effect, those who blame themselves experience psychological threat (and real threat, probably), while those who blame the system experience only real threat. The alternative forms of threat are consequences of the ascription of blame, however, and not identical to it. The inmates in Bettleheim's account did not, typically, blame themselves for their difficulties. Nonetheless, they experienced psychological threat.

Status Threat

Thus far we have discussed responses to extreme threat of a physical sort. Such threats rarely occur, even in the harshest of American prisons. Our discussion of threat will focus on threats to the inmate's or to the staff's status. What types of social relations are status-giving and what types are status-degrading?

The description of social class by Warner, along with many others, have stressed what may be called a "local" view of status. In Warner's analysis, status is conferred by a social group for possessing whatever local attribute happens to be admired. He rejects the notion that money is necessary to upper-class position and gives numerous examples to the contrary.[16] Other students of social status argue that there are some relatively universal attributes which are related to status in most social groups, and whose absence will cause a decline in status in the long run.

A wide variety of research supports the proposition that "he who has control has status; he who loses control loses status." W. F. Whyte's study of the restaurant documents the cook's need to assert his control in a situation in which natural control lay in the hands of the waitresses.[17] Caplow suggests that the primary dimension along which occupational esteem is evaluated is the amount of control exercised over self and others.[18] This principle has been formalized by industrial sociologists in the notion that higher status positions must initiate interactions in order to avoid tension.[19]

An interesting experimental example is offered by Bavelas in a comparison of the star and circle pattern of communication in problem solving. In the star pattern all communication flowed through a central "leader" who solved the problem; in the circle pattern there was no leader and the problem was solved collectively. A good deal of innovation was displayed in the circle pattern, but the star showed no innovation at all. The leader resisted all attempts to introduce new ideas. To accept new ideas from the members on the periphery would be to surrender the control and lose status.[20]

Control and Exchange

Thus we see that control is an important component of social status, and is for that reason important to most people. The preceding research suggests that there are many subtle ways in which control is established. One way in which inferences as to control are made is in a bargaining or negotiation situation. If A continually gets more than B in his bargaining -- if B does not get reciprocity -- we conclude that A has bent B to his will.

The situation described by McCleery in our discussion of rational approaches can be analyzed in the above terms. In the older, custody-oriented institutions the

-25-

exchange of values between staff and inmates was at least not unfavorable to inmates. In exchange for peace and order, the inmates received rather important privileges -- access to good jobs and various illegal services. In some prisons the illegal services are said to be quite extensive and include alcohol, narcotics, and even women; if not the latter, then permission for homosexual relationships. Illegal services are important because, among other reasons, they are things that the staff do not wish to give. This in itself makes them valuable as symbols of power. As the new treatment-oriented staff took over, they had quite a different conception of a proper exchange. No illegal services were to be provided, and the inmate now needed to exchange more than good behavior for privileges. He had to exchange his identity for the privileges, i.e., become "rehabilitated" in order to get a soft job. Such an exchange seems highly unfavorable to the inmate. To engage in the new exchange arrangements would clearly establish the dominance of the staff.

The concept *exchange* plays a very important part of the work of George C. Homans.[21] Drawing from learning theory and economics, Homans offers a great many propositions about exchange behavior. Primarily, however, Homans examines the motivational properties of exchange. He is concerned with explaining whey people of different statuses do, or do not, make any specific exchange. For Homans, status is one of the investments an individual makes, for which rewards are expected in return. In the present theory, we are examining status as if it were a *consequence* of the exchanges that are made. In one chapter of *The Human Group*, Homans deals with social conflict.[22] He examines the case of the design engineers in one plant who lose their capacity to initiate interaction and thereby lose status. A limited amount of conflict between the engineers and the supervisors ensues. Here, Homans is stating a case in very similar terms to those above. Although Homans does not pursue the discussion formally, it is of some interest that the only example of conflict that he chose was concerned with status. We have argued that status is a key variable in the explanation of conflict. What is the peculiar property of status threat, if any, as compared to many objective deprivations related to food, shelter, amusement, etc?

When an individual is deprived of money, or amusement, there are a great many things he can do to gain these gratifications that are not inherently threatening to others. He can work overtime, or quit his job. Status threats, on the other hand, lead him to attempt to restructure his relationship to others in ways that are likely to become threatening to the statuses of the others. Thus, status threat is likely to induce a response from the other that quickly creates a conscious antagonism between the parties. The threatened party may even withdraw from objective gratifications, in order to maintain a favorable exchange relationship. He becomes concerned with reducing the gratifications he is providing for certain others, and less concerned with doubtful attemps to increase his own gratifications.

Dominance and Mock Behavior

There are a variety of ways to cope with demands for an unfavorable exchange relationship. For example, one can *behave* like a rehabilitated inmate, while mocking treatment goals, i.e., one may establish "role distance" to use Goffman's term.[22] By establishing role distance, a mechanism is evolved for undervaluing what is being invested in the exchange. Milosz offers a very insightful analysis of the defensive properties of mock behavior, which he calls "Ketman."[24] His concern is with the citizens of totalitarian states, but in prisons one can find many inmates who deal with the threat created by staff demands by means of "Ketman." These inmates artfully deceive the staff into the belief that they are loyal and willing subjects. To such inmates, the very willingness of the staff to accept mock behavior becomes a glorious proof of the staff's stupidity and the inmate's sophistication. Such "passive manipulation" of the staff, although occasionally it can receive group support, is only available to certain kinds of inmates. Most of McCleery's inmates dealt with the situation by beginning the spiral of conflict.

Dominance and Withdrawal Behavior

McCleery's analysis of status in Oahu prison presented a dilemma to us. McCleery found that inmate leaders who supported the staff's desire for a "Cool" institution were admired, but also that inmates who rejected staff demands and stood up to punishment without breaking were also admired. For the adaptive "norm" of order, both the conformers and the deviators were admired.

As we have said, the inmate leaders at Oahu maintained a favorable exchange balance. They received privileges in return for the promise of stability. Furthermore, they displayed a thorough contempt for the staff. The contempt was not just "showing off" to other inmates. It indicated to other inmates that the leaders had not rewarded the staff by giving them a shift of attitude in return for the privileges. Thus, the inmate leader kept his socially visible "payments" to the staff at a minimum and his status at a maximum.

The inmate leader maintains his status image by creating a favorable "balance of payments" with the staff; the inmate who "stands up to punishment" maintains status by refusing to negotiate. To maintain status, an inmate need not receive anything. As long as he gives nothing, he maintains an exchange balance: zero equals zero. What the inmates admired at Oahu prison was neither conformity to the "norm" of stability, nor deviation from it. <u>They admired inmates who were able to get at least as much from the system as they gave to it.</u>

An inmate at one prison was describing his relationship with a correctional officer:

> I had this experience with this officer in one situation; it was unconstitutional, I think. I went and picked up my newspaper one day -- it came in the mail, you know -- and this screw (correctional officer) got all red in the face and got buggy-eyed, as buggy-eyed as you can get, and told me to "put that God damn paper down and leave it alone." I told him, "It's got my name on it, it's got my cell on it, I'll save you a trip downstairs, I'll take it now." So he repeated himself -- he was screaming at me -- "Put that God damn paper down and I'll pass it up." So I came in and told him, after chow, that I thought I'd go to the hole (isolation).

The quoted individual was an inmate who was deeply motivated to "go straight." An habitual offender sentence loomed as an ominous possibility. From his point of view, the staff held many important rewards in their possession: early parole, help in getting another state to drop previous charges, etc. But suddenly he found himself involved in a degrading interaction with an officer. To continue behaving the way the staff wanted him to, in the face of this very negative return, would create a highly unfavorable exchange balance. <u>A nasty officer is not inherently threatening to one's status; he is threatening only if one is conforming to staff demands.</u>

What is the inmate's way of resolving the problem? He says, in effect, "Send me to the hole. I will withdraw from negotiation with the staff. You give me nothing and I'll give you nothing. Thus I'll maintain my status."

Dominance and the Perceived Sources of Action

To say that individual A is exercising control over individual B is an interpretation of events. It is an interpretation of A's response to certain demands that are made upon him. To answer the question of how A makes inferences as to the amount of control he maintains, we have to ask how he will interpret the demands made upon him. There are three ways in which demands on a person can arise. They can arise because of what he perceives to be his own wishes, because of the demands of the alter with whom he interacts, or finally because of some forces arising outside the interaction with alter. This outside force may be a third party or perhaps some entirely impersonal force such as the climate.

The reduction of conflict by the use of superordinate goals can be analyzed in terms of the preceding notions of exchange and the sources of demands. Superordinate goals constitute a rational motivation for reduction of conflict. As we have pointed out, strong rational motivations do not always reduce conflict, because to act rationally may require an exchange which threatens the individual self-esteem. If the response of the <u>other</u> to an unfavorable exchange is to assume that ego has acquiesced in the power struggle, the other may demand an increasingly more unfavorable exchange. Thus, what seems to be a rational motivation is not rational at all in terms of the symbols of dominance -- which have <u>become</u> quite real to the system participants.

Superordinate goals have a different character and alter the whole nature of the exchange relation. There were two groups of boys in Sherif's camp, the Eagles and the Rattlers. If the Eagles, for example, asked the Rattlers to help locate a stoppage in the water line that affected the whole camp, this need not be seen in dominance terms. The Rattlers need not see their accession to the request as an exchange because they were likely to do the job in consequence of its <u>value to themselves</u>. The source of the demand becomes ego, not alter. Alternatively, it may be said that the source of the demand is a third party to the transaction, namely, the water supply! Superordinate goals have an impersonal character in that they stem from the situation and not from the demands of others. Acting toward the achievement of the goal does not necessarily assert alter's dominance. How far this argument can be carried is an open question. The perspective may be so narrowly focused, and the demand of the opponent may be delivered in such a provoking manner that the individual may display the well-known reaction of "cutting off his nose to spite his face." Anything his opponent wishes is to be resisted.

Wheeler found that most inmates approve of an inmate's going to a therapy program. Since so many other forms of "giving in" to the staff are disapproved by the inmates, such a finding requires explanation. Wheeler suggested that inmate approval was contingent upon avoidance of "brown-nosing." Inmates make a rather clear differentiation between those inmates who are sincere in their efforts to improve themselves and those who support pro-social values ... (to gain) early release, or an easy job."[25] When an inmate goes into a therapy program only because the staff wants him to, he is behaving in a subordinate manner. When he does the same thing because <u>he wants to</u>, it is no longer seen as submissive behavior. Refusing to hide money for a fellow inmate, on the other hand, is prima pacie evidence of submission since an inmate can make the assumption that no other inmate believes that having money is really wrong. A third example of this phenomenon is suggested by McCleery's analysis of the conditions which terminate a riot -- "anarchy is its own best answer." As we have suggested, riot conditions have such negative consequences <u>for the inmates themselves</u> that the inmates may come to see its termination as something they are doing, not to please the staff but to please themselves. Riot leaders attack other inmates, commit homosexual aggressions, etc.[26] If the staff can refrain from provocative acts that reassert the old dominance symbols, the inmates will probably end the riot of their own will, though not without making "exchange capital" out of it.

<u>Dominance, Exchange, and the Perceived Sources of Action</u>

Two further propositions can now be offered.

5. An unbalanced exchange relationship is a symbol of the dominance of the favored party.

6. If self, or an external party or event is seen as the source of the demands on oneself, the transaction is not perceived as an exchange, thus losing its meaning as an assertion of dominance.

Simmel points out that in the act of accepting defeat the vanquished makes a gift to the victor. Such an act is felt by the victor to be "a sort of offense." In this voluntary character of declaring oneself vanquished lies an ultimate proof of one's power."[27] While the point seems overstated, it is clear thay by laying down arms before he has to, the defeated declares himself out of the negotiation process. He submits voluntarily, and self becomes the source of the act, not the other. In this sense, the defeated is like the therapists of Pioneer House who refused to validate the child's conception of his own aggression as acts of dominance over the staff.

<u>Negotiated Reward as a Style of Life</u>

Much has been written about the threatening character of the early stages of institutionalization. The process of "stripping" or "mortification" has been described by Goffman with great clarity.[28] The inmate is forced to make very unbalanced exchanges, such as saying "pretty please" to get a cigarette or defiling himself in return for not getting beaten. Such extreme self-defilement, as we have indicated, seems to produce great psychological threat. But even if the inmate manages to maintain his self-esteem during the mortification process, even if in the "progressive" prison there is no mortification process, there is a special character to institutional life which creates "real threat" and prompts the inmate to evaluate all behavior in the dominance dimension. This is what can be called "the negotiated character of reward" as the special style of total institutions. Everything must be bought. It is common aphorism among correctional officials, both custody and treatment, that privileges must be earned; as it turns out, everything is a privilege. Such a principle does not characterize normal social systems. One does not deny one's child the right to go to school because of some slight misbehavior. A supervisor does not deny the worker his wages because he feels that the worker has not been doing a full day's work (although he may eventually fire him). Short-range negotiation for one's daily essentials and even one's luxuries is not normally necessary; one gets most of these things as a kind of right, or as a result of long-range bargains which cannot be cancelled on a moment's notice. Negotiations, we have argued, serve as a symbol of domination if one of the parties is underprivileged. We can now add another proposition. We have argued that unfavorable exchange tends to create a threat to self-esteem. Negotiated reward as a style of institutional life has two effects. It tends to create higher threat to the self-image than when the negotiation is less frequent, by its continual reminders of the dominance of the staff. Second, negotiated reward tends to move the individuals on to the dominance dimension more totally. This is true for both inmate and staff since it reminds the staff of his dominance over the inmate and the inmate of his domination by the staff.

7a. Negotiated reward reinforces the tendency to conceptualize interaction in terms of dominance.

7b. Negotiated reward tends to cause threat to the inmate's self-esteem and thus encourages him to counterattack.

7c. Since the staff responds to the counterattack (especially since interaction is conceptualized in dominance terms), a state of conflict between the parties ensues. <u>Negotiated reward leads to more or less continual conflict behavior.</u>

One of the efforts of the more radical penal institutions, such as the Highfields Project, or the California Institution for Men at Chino, has been to reduce the negotiated character of interaction. The Highfields staff told their charges that many former privileges were now to be considered rights. Visits to town could not be withdrawn for the usual run of misconduct (although inmates could be sent away). Although the usual penal official would shudder at the thought of giving up his "tools," the Highfield staff claims that shucking off their power in this way reduced misconduct.[29]

McCleery makes note of the large number of assaults between inmates in the period of conflict of Oahu prison.[30] Negotiated reward is almost as much a principle of interaction between inmates as it is between inmates and staff, especially during a period in which traditional leadership has crumbled. For this reason the symbols of dominance may become salient in inmate interaction. While inmates are not normally disprivileged in their exchanges with other inmates, one can explain the higher assault rate (and the high assault rate in prisons generally) as a result of operating primarily on the dominance dimension.

FOOTNOTES

[1] Ralf Dahrendorf, Class and Class Conflict in an Industrial Society (Stanford, Calif.: Stanford University Press, 1959), p. 135.

[2] Kenneth E. Boulding, Conflict and Defense (New York: Harper and Brothers, 1962), p. 5.

[3] Robert E. Park and Ernest W. Burgess, Introduction to the Science of Sociology (Chicago: University of Chicago Press, 1921; second edition, 1924), p. 510.

[4] Richard Cloward, discussant in Helen Leland Witmer and Ruth Kotinsky (eds.), New Perspectives for Research on Juvenile Delinquency (Washington, D.C.: United States Department of Health, Education, and Welfare, Children's Bureau Publication No. 356, 1956), p. 88.

[5] Muzafer Sherif, et al., Intergroup Conflict and Cooperation: The Robber's Cave Experiment (Norman, Oklahoma: Institute of Group Relations, University of Oklahoma, 1961).

[6] Kenyon J. Scudder, Prisoners are People (New York: Doubleday, 1952), pp. 14-16.

[7] James S. Coleman, Community Conflict (Glencoe, Ill.: The Free Press, 1957), p. 11, footnote.

[8] Lewis A. Coser, "The Termination of Conflict," The Journal of Conflict Resolution, V:4 (December, 1961), 347-353.

[9] Bruno Bettleheim, "Individual and Mass Behavior in Crisis Situations," Journal of Abnormal and Social Psychology, XXXVIII (October, 1943), 425.

[10] Eugen Kogon, The Theory and Practice of Hell (New York: Berkeley, 1960), Chapter 20, "The Underground Struggle."

[11] Fritz Redl and David Wineman, Children Who Hate (New York: The Free Press, 1951), p. 48.

[12] Ibid., p. 120.

[13] T.W. Adorno, et al., The Authoritarian Personality (New York: Harper and Brothers, 1950). See the discussion of the high degree of power orientation of the authoritarian subjects on p. 478 and the discussion of their extensive dependency needs on p. 449. Many of the authoritarian subjects showed considerable submission to their parents, who were often feared.

[14] Bettleheim, op. cit., p. 429.

[15] Richard A. Cloward and Lloyd E. Ohlin, Delinquency and Opportunity (Glencoe, Ill.: The Free Press, 1960), pp. 110-113.

[16] W. Lloyd Warner, Marchia Meeker, and Kenneth Eells, Social Class in America (Chicago: Science Research Associates, 1949), p. 8.

[17] William F. Whyte, "Social Structure of the Organization: The Restaurant" in Robert Dubin (ed.), Human Relations in Administration (New York: Prentice-Hall, 1951).

[18] Theodore Caplow, The Sociology of Work (Minneapolis: University of Minnesota Press, 1954), p. 52. "There does seem to be one property of an occupational position which correlates almost perfectly with the rank order of prestige ratings. I have called this element behavior control: the position of the subject with respect to the control of other people's behavior, and their control of his."

[19] William F. Whyte, "Industrial Sociology" in Joseph B. Gittler (ed.), Review of Sociology: Analysis of a Decade (New York: Wiley, 1957), p. 300.

[20] Alex Bavelas, Proceedings of the Third Annual Seminar on Social Science for Industry: Motivation (Menlo Park, Calif.: Stanford Research Institute), pp. 29-30.

[21] George C. Homans, Social Behavior: Its Elementary Forms (New York: Harcourt Brace and Co., 1961); The Human Group (New York: Harcourt Brace and Co., 1950).

[22] Homans, The Human Group, ibid., Chapter 15.

[23] Erving Goffman, Encounters (Indianapolis, Ind.: Bobbs-Merrill Co., 1961), p. 108.

[24] Czeslaw Milosz, The Captive Mind (New York: Knopf, 1953).

[25] Stanton Wheeler, "Social Organization in a Correctional Community," (unpublished Ph.D. dissertation, University of Washington, Seattle, 1958), p. 56.

[26] Clarence C. Schrag, "The Sociology of Prison Riots," in Proceedings of the American Correctional Association (New York: American Correctional Association, 1960), p. 141.

[27] George Simmel, Conflict and the Web of Group Affiliations (Glencoe, Ill.: The Free Press, 1955), p. 114.

[28] Erving Goffman, Asylums (New York: Anchor Books, 1961), pp. 14-48.

[29] Lloyd W. McCorkle, Albert Eliss, and F. Lovell Bixby, *The Highfields Story* (New York: Henry Holt and Co., 1958), p. 27.

[30] Richard H. McCleery, "The Governmental Process and Informal Social Control" in Donald R. Cressey (ed.), *The Prison* (New York: Holt, Rinehart, and Winston, 1961), p. 179.

CHAPTER III

THE INTERPERSONAL ENVIRONMENT AND CONFLICT

The discussion has been sketched primarily in terms of social-psychological processes, on the one hand, and broad structural factors that may create a propensity for conflict, on the other. In looking for explanations of the variation in degree of conflict behavior among inmates, the variation in the social milieu may be of great importance. How does the social environment relate to the propositions we have discussed?

THE EFFECTS OF CULTURE ON CONFLICT

Earlier we discussed the notion that cultural difference creates a propensity for conflict--a proposition we found wanting. One of the ways in which normative differences may create a conflict is suggested by proposition six, which stated that demands which are seen as originating from the self are not symbols of dominance or submission. One of the effects of differences in social background or normative affiliation is to make for a relatively large number of situations in which the demands made by B for A are seen by A as alien demands, as B's wishes and not A's. If the cultural difference were "complete," no superordinate goals would be possible, since there would be nothing that A and B jointly value. It is in this sense that culture creates a potentiality for conflict. In the prison, however, we should be aware of a possibility that this assertion is tautological. The so-called inmate culture, in many aspects, may be a result of pre-existing conflict. The things valued by this culture may be chosen primarily for their significance as symbols of defiance of the staff.

THE INFORMATIONAL ASPECTS OF THE SOCIAL MILIEU

One of the major arguments in the present formulation is the nation that dominance is asserted by an unfavorable exchange relation between staff and inmate. What can the staff exchange that is of value? One can give privileges: cigarettes, jobs, books, visitors, letters from home. Most of these are of little value or cost to the staff. Giving these in return for things highly regarded by the inmate creates an unfavorable exchange for the inmate. But the staff can give something of far greater value if it is willing to shift its own attitudes. A staff member can come to positively value an inmate, sympathize with the inmate's concerns, and modify his own behavior, the rules, and other such things to suit the inmate. If the inmate behaves nicely for a sympathetic staff, he is not making an unfavorable exchange; if he accommodates to an unsympathetic staff, he is making a highly unfavorable exchange. A good example of this kind of problem for inmates was given the author by an insightful prisoner.

> Inmate: One of the ideas you often hear around here is "never cop out" (admit one's guilt). If you get caught with a smoking revolver in your hand, standing over the body, claim you just picked it up!
>
> Author: How about going before the classification committee for a rule infraction? Isn't it possible they'd go lighter if you frankly admitted your guilt?
>
> Inmate: They probably would, but then they might throw the book at you, too. And that would bother the hell out of me and make me feel like a damn fool.

If the inmate "cops out," he makes a very damaging admission about himself; he does just what the staff wants him to do and puts himself in their power. He gives something of great value. If he gets mistreated in exchange, if the staff uses the situation to attack him rather than coming to see him as an honest person who deserves decent treatment, he experiences a feeling of great subordination--"I'd feel like a damn fool." This suggests a principle: never make extreme accommodations unless you are sure of a fair exchange.

The inmate's friends and associates give him some idea of what he can get from the staff in the way of specific privileges, but he will find out many of these things for himself. Much less clear from the inmate's direct experience are the kinds of major concessions the staff may make. What will the parole board do? What will the classification committee do? What do the staff members say about convicts behind their backs; how do they really feel about them? These are questions that may be largely answered for the inmate by his fellow inmates. Let us assume that his associates assert that the staff is extremely unsympathetic. He need not like his associates or wish to share their values to accept the validity of the information they provide. Once he has accepted these assertions, he will come to view the accommodation he is asked to make to the staff as an unfavorable exchange, especially if the accommodation involves an attitude change on his part.

What we are suggesting here is a way to explain certain aspects of inmate conformity. If the staff is defined as unsympathetic and if certain acts are defined as submission to the staff, the inmate is constrained to refuse the performance of those acts. Initially, such "misbehavior" should not be taken as willful conformity to the inmate culture. The inmate may not express hostility toward the staff because he wishes to show he is a loyal inmate.

There is a second way in which the social milieu may provide information that serves to control inmate responses. Other inmates can articulate a picture of staff responses to dominance behavior by the inmate group.

Coser suggests that conflict is functional for the group; others have suggested that it relieves boredom. The pictures of the often extreme consequences of conflict that have been presented herein should suggest that conflict is not always fun for the participants. The inmate group can minimize the negative response from the staff-- they can portray the staff as weak (but not sympathetic and tolerant); they can offer evidence that the staff can be manipulated by brute force. In a study of a politically oriented voluntary association, it was shown that conflict-oriented members tended to argue that others could be manipulated by fear and tended to disagree that attitude change was necessary to the accomplishment of organizational goals.[1] If one starts with the belief that to change the staff one must change their attitudes, one is restrained from provocative behavior. But even if the inmate believes that it _is_ necessary to change staff attitudes, he can argue that a riot will arouse the civilians against the staff and thus force a change in attitudes. He has made conflict functional, in his view of things.[2] Schrag has noted that civilian support for the plight of inmates will tend to touch off new waves of rioting; in the South, where less civilian support is felt, self-destructive tactics are the usual method of counter-attacking the staff.[3]

A relatively tightly knit inmate group, containing few inmates oriented toward non-conflict tactics, can minimize the dysfunctional consequences of conflict. When very high power is concentrated in the hands of the staff, it may be only such unique groups that can create the belief that conflict will be fun.

THE SOCIAL MILIEU CAN PROVIDE AN AUDIENCE

It is a sociological aphorism that some things are more disturbing to individuals when done publicly than when done privately. Facts that disagree with the public presentation of self are most dangerous when they become known and thus attack that presentation. In many areas, it is primarily the publicly presented self, rather than the private self, that is important. It seems plausible that this is the case in dominance behavior. To accommodate to the staff may be far more disturbing in front of an inmate audience than when done in private. Again, the distinction between real threat and psychological threat may be involved. If the prospective submission might create belief that one is _unable_ to fight back, then an act of submission cannot be readily carried out even in privacy or away from the inmate audience. On the other hand, an act of submission which creates a real threat but not a psychological one is more degrading as a public act than a private one. The inmate may be like the married man who is quite willing to do the dishes so long as his friends are not around and his wife has the good sense to refrain from making this behavior known.

The necessity to publicly avoid accommodation is an alternative and quite plausible explanation of the "pluralistic ignorance" Wheeler[4] and Cloward[5] refer to. They argue that inmates will often not act in ways that are conforming to staff expectations only because they fail to understand the degree of inmate acceptance of the act. Wheeler presented hypothetical situations in which acts of conformity to staff were depicted and asked inmates to indicate whether they approved of the behavior or not and also to indicate how other inmates might respond. The _typical_ inmate saw others as less approving of conformity to the staff than he was. In truth, most inmates

-36-

shared his private attitudes toward the staff. A next logical step is to conclude that if inmates were aware of others' opinions, they would conform to staff expectations.

But as Wheeler indicates, approval does not mean that the inmate wants to do the thing in question; most inmates approved the hypothetical inmate's desire to join a group therapy program even though they felt no need of group therapy. Approval does not have a self referent, necessarily. What the inmate may be saying is, "I don't mind if others accommodate, but I won't be publicly submissive." One may not mind one's friend allowing himself to be henpecked.

If one found out that the others approve, the act might still retain its degrading character, as long as the act was public, as long as it has an audience. The low visibility of pro-staff opinion may be a consequence, and not a cause, of the reluctance of inmates to engage in accommodative behavior.

In Chapter I we discussed the case of the inmate "follower" who will not negotiate with the staff, even though he may be pleased when the inmate leaders "make deals." When the leader negotiates, he is often in a position to create a new definition of the situation. The leader can publicly define the exchange as a favorable one, so that everyone in the group becomes aware that the leader is not subordinating himself to the staff. The follower is less often in a position to so define the situation. It may be acceptable to publicly accommodate, when the transaction has been publicly defined as a favorable one; it may become publicly degrading to accommodate when the transaction is favorable only by a private definition.

WHAT IS THE EFFECT OF CONFLICT ON THE SOCIAL MILIEU?

Coser, drawing his material from Simmel, points out that conflict often unites unrelated persons and groups.[6] Their interests may have been antagonistic in the past, but the need for defense against a common enemy often creates coalitions that become the real groups of the future. Marx tried to explain the ability of these temporary coalitions to develop solid roots. He saw class consciousness as a result of class conflict and not its cause.

> As long as the rule of the bourgeois class had not organized itself fully, the opposition of the other classes could not come forth in its pure form either . . . . Increasingly (as a result of conflicts within the productive sphere) the collisions between the individual worker and the individual bourgeois assume the character of collisions between two classes.[7]

As the bourgeois begins to respond to the worker as an enemy, the worker begins to identify with other members of the working class. In a very different sphere of behavior, Charles Fritz gives us an analysis of how the intimacy develops between formerly antagonistic individuals as a result of exposure to a common enemy.[8] In Fritz's material the common enemy is a natural disaster. The disaster creates the unique feeling that all others are sharing the same anxieties, the same blow of fate. No one is dominant; no one is master or subordinate because all have been laid low by the holocaust.

Fritz quotes a psychiatrist who treated (one would assume, medically) disaster victims:

> They were not like a regular accident victim. It was so much a part of such a big thing, there was a transient loss of individuality and identification with something else.[9]

Fritz points out that:

> Culturally derived discriminations and social distinctions tend to be eliminated in a disaster because all groups and statuses in the society are indiscriminately affected.[10]

Three weeks after a devastating tornado, the inhabitants of Judsonia, Arkansas, were asked a series of questions about their overall sense of deprivation. Over three-quarters of those interviewed said they had not suffered great deprivation (of 1,100 people, 435 were killed or injured, and virtually every house was destroyed). When asked to compare their suffering to others, over half felt they had suffered less than others; and not a single person felt more deprived.[11] An overwhelming sense of identification develops, communication is facilitated, and people can further explore and solidify their tentative feeling that "the other fellow is just like me."

The feeling of being attacked by the guards is one factor which welds the inmates as a group. It does not necessarily produce positive sentiments about the group, as we shall attempt to show.

SUMMARY OF THE THEORY OF CONFLICT

A series of theoretical statements and research cases were examined in an attempt to derive a highly general theory of conflict. A number of propositions were formulated, related to a limited number of variables. In summary, two major themes were stressed. First, it was argued that status threat led to conflict behavior. Second, it was argued that when participants in a relationship view the interaction in dominance terms, conflict is likely to ensue. These two propositions are highly interrelated. For example, when status threat is experienced, it is likely that the party or parties will come to view the interaction in dominance terms. Conversely, when the interaction is viewed by the parties in dominance terms, it is likely that one or more of the participants will come to experience status threat. Other factors related to threat and dominance were considered.

Although some fairly concrete assertions have been made, we have avoided highly specific predictions about prison behavior. The operational referents of many of the concepts have been investigated too little to allow for crucial tests of the propositions. The research will be exploratory, designed to add evidence for the relevance of the propositions and to increase or decrease confidence in their validity.

FOOTNOTES

[1] George S. Rothbart, "Ideology and Strategy: A Study of Attitudes toward the Organizational Process" (unpublished Master's thesis, University of Washington, Seattle, 1962), pp. 148-151.

[2] See a parallel in ibid., pp. 151-152.

[3] Clarence C. Schrag, "The Sociology of Prison Riots" in *Proceedings of the American Correctional Association* (New York: American Correctional Association, 1960), pp. 138 and 146.

[4] Stanton Wheeler, "Social Organization in a Correctional Community" (unpublished Ph.D. dissertation, University of Washington, Seattle, 1958), p. 85.

[5] Richard A. Cloward, *New Perspectives for Research on Juvenile Delinquency* (Washington, D.C.: Children's Bureau Publication No. 356, 1956), pp. 80-91.

[6] Lewis Coser, *The Functions of Social Conflict* (Glencoe, Ill.: The Free Press, 1956), Chapter 8.

[7] Ralf Dahrendorf (trans.), *Class and Class Conflict in Industrial Society* (Stanford, Calif.: Stanford University Press, 1959), p. 16.

[8] Charles E. Fritz, "Disaster" in Robert K. Merton and Robert A. Nisbet (eds.), *Contemporary Social Problems* (New York: Harcourt, Brace and World, 1961), Chapter 14.

[9] Ibid., p. 687.

[10] Ibid., p. 685.

[11] Eli S. Marks, Charles E. Fritz, et al., "Human Reactions in Disaster Situations" (unpublished report, National Opinion Research Center, University of Chicago, June, 1954), Vol. I, p. 222.

CHAPTER IV

THE RESEARCH DESIGN

THE SETTING

The research reported here was done at Western State Reformatory,[1] a pseudonym for the same institution studied earlier by Stanton Wheeler.[2] Our aim was to gather a variety of data on attitude, behavior, and social position which are relevant to the theory of conflict described earlier.

Western State Reformatory is a prison for youthful offenders, most of whom vary in agr from 17 to 25 years old. The physical design of the institution is traditional: concrete walls, gun towers, and the old-fashioned type of inside cell construction designed to make inmates highly visible to the staff and to prevent escape. Nonetheless, the institution aims to be primarily oriented toward rehabilitation. An academic school covering all elementary and secondary grades is well equipped with classroom and laboratory facilities and a fully qualified civilian teaching staff. The institution maintains many vocational schools, offering training in printing, carpentry, auto mechanics, drafting, barbering, etc. Except for the physical construction of the institution, life at Western State Reformatory is less harsh than in many prisons. In his leisure time, the inmate can read books from the library, watch television, and participate in numerous social activities. So many clubs and hobby activities are available to the inmate that such activities were serious obstacles to getting inmates to show up at our questionnaire sessions.

Due to liberal parole policies in Western State, inmates at this institution serve relatively short sentences. Those inmates committed for crimes where a long sentence is fixed by law are frequently sent to the custody-oriented penitentiary in the state. The average length of stay for inmates paroled from the Reformatory in 1962 was 18.9 months.[3] Thus, the Reformatory has a high turnover. Many inmates had been within the walls only a brief time, and a large number were shortly due to leave. Furthermore, inmates were frequently transferred to the honor farm and the forest camps within the state. This situation of high turnover may be contrasted to the State Penitentiary. At the Penitentiary most inmates serve relatively long sentences. Although the liberal parole policy affects this institution, parole is less liberal for older inmates with a long criminal record, who thereby tend to accumulate in the Penitentiary population. The Penitentiary had a median length of stay of 20.4 months for inmates paroled in 1962. During 1962, 25.4 percent of the parolees from the Penitentiary had served a commitment of over 36 months, while only 7.6 percent of the parolees from the Reformatory had served that much time.[4]

According to staff members and others familiar with both institutions, the different degrees of turnover in population tend to be reflected in the respective social climates. At the Penitentiary, relations between inmates tend to be stable and a rapprochement between guards and inmates is said to exist and be enforced by inmate opinion. Conversely, the situation at the Reformatory is said to involve much flux in interpersonal relations within the inmate group and between inmates and guards. The staff describes the Reformatory as a much "hotter" institution than the Penitentiary. Disturbances in the Reformatory arise readily, but dissipate as readily. The Penitentiary, on the other hand, is said to be slow to boil, but, once heated conflict arises, it is of a deadly serious and persistent nature.

The foregoing parallels McCleery's analysis of Oahu prison,[5] discussed earlier, as well as Cloward's discussion of a military prison.[6] Both authors found that stable social structure is accompanied by less frequent conflict.

THE SAMPLE

Our plan was to gather data on a variety of different variables related to the previously outlined theory. Most of the propositions explicitly relate to change in degree of conflict behavior. Thus it was desirable to test these propositions by using repeated questionnaires over a period of time, on a panel of inmates.

Ideally, the panel should consist of a group of inmates, taken at the time of their arrival and followed through their entire institutional careers. Because of time limitations, such a possibility was not open to us. A number of other choices were available. We could select a group of inmates at their arrival and follow them for a brief period of time. However, previous studies have suggested that the impact of an institution is quite different at different points in the inmate's sentence.[7] Thus we would have data appropriate only to "early" inmates if we chose the last-mentioned alternative. In fact, it was important to us to examine the effect of time on the attitudes and behavior being studied. Another choice of panels was the possibility of using inmates from a similar position in the formal structure of the prison--inmates from one cell block, or one work unit, or all from the school, etc. The effect of the reciprocities available in each of these positions could then be examined in detail. Again, our interest was in examining the effect of differences in position, just as we wished to examine the effect of _differences_ in time.

It was decided to draw a sample as close to representative as possible, since such a sample would provide us with the maximum opportunity to compare a variety of different factors.

Part of the study, to be described in Chapter IX, involved discussion groups designed to change attitudes and behavior. In order to be able to participate in these discussion groups, an inmate had to be within the walls, and out of the reception and guidance unit. For this reason, we eliminated individuals from those units for selection into the panel to be discussed herein. In addition, life outside the walls or in the reception and guidance unit was so different from that of the "mainline" inmates as to preclude any combined analysis. One further selection criterion was used. To be included, the inmates should not be scheduled for discharge within six months of the beginning of the study. One final questionnaire, a follow-up on the present study, was to be given shortly before the end of that time period. Of course, such a criterion meant that our initial questionnaire responses would include no one scheduled for immediate discharge. However, the "aging" of our sample would eventually produce such persons.

To summarize the sample criteria:

1. It was to be, in general, representative. It was not necessary that it be perfectly representative. To do the kinds of analyses we wished, it should be approximately representative.

2. Inmates from outside the walls--the honor farm crew--or from the reception and guidance unit were eliminated.

3. Inmates with less than six months to serve were eliminated.

The initial sample consisted of 170 inmates, who were to receive three questionnaires over a period of three months. There was some loss of respondents between questionnaires, and the third questionnaire included 125 of the original 170 inmates. The three questionnaires were administered at the following approximate dates:

First questionnaire - June 26
Second questionnaire - August 1
Third questionnaire - September 20

For a variety of reasons some inmates were given questionnaires before these dates. Gathering in the recalcitrant respondents tended to prolong the questionnaire administration for about a week after the above dates.

Drawing the Initial Sample

In this prison, inmates are assigned to caseworkers by rotation, in the order in which they arrive in the institution. Although exceptions are occasionally made, individuals who arrive together are not assigned to the same caseworker but are distributed between the different caseworkers. Caseworkers have an approximately equal case load. Thus each caseworker's list of inmates approximates a systematic or successive sample of inmates in the institution. To draw our initial sample we used the entire lists of two caseworkers supplemented by a systematic sample from a third list. A small number (under 10) were disqualified due to low I.Q. or illiteracy.

These lists provided us with 356 names. We then sent a note to each of these inmates explaining the purposes of the study. This note is reproduced in Appendix A. The note stressed three things:

1. Participation was voluntary. If the inmate wished to participate, he

should return the attached slip.

2. The inmate would be paid from one to four dollars for his participation, the specific amount depending on the number of things he would be asked to do. He did not know how much he would be asked to do.

3. Although the inmate would be asked to give his institutional number, the responses would be absolutely confidential and no member of the staff or the State Department of Institutions would "ever" be able to look at his responses. The note was signed by a sociologist on the staff of the Reformatory, who acted in the role of "research coordinator." For emphasis, the research coordinator pointed out that _he_ would not be able to look at the responses.

We received 200 volunteer slips, of which 170 took the first questionnaire. The 30 initial non-respondents included a few persons whose schedules could not be fitted into the planned sequence of questionnaires or discussion groups. Mostly, the non-respondents were individuals who did not show up for the first session, even though they had been notified of a time and place to which they had been assigned. When the 170 inmates showed up to take the first questionnaire, we briefly explained that the purpose of the study was to better understand inmate attitudes. We repeated our original statement that participation was voluntary, and added that if they began the study we would expect them to complete the four questionnaires to be given over the next six months; (the fourth questionnaire is a follow-up not reported herein).

The inmates were told that if the series was not finished, we would not be able to use their questionnaires and therefore would not be able to pay them. All 170 inmates agreed to begin participation.

Characteristics of the Sample

Tables I and II present the data on initial and subsequent participation in the panel.

It should not be assumed that all 170 inmates who began the panel were equally enthusiastic and anxious to continue their participation. At the time of the first questionnaire session, an inmate who wished to withdraw would have to do so in the presence of a staff member. Some of the later drop-outs were probably initially reluctant, but avoided open expression of their feelings at the first session and chose the more quiet technique of later withdrawal.

Nonetheless, many factors other than reluctance account for drop-out. One who has not carried out a panel study can hardly imagine the difficulties of getting people to appear repeatedly to fill out questionnaires. Merely keeping track of 170 people is a difficult task, even in the closed society of a prison. Certain kinds of jobs made inmates unavailable, other leisure activities interfered with their attendance, many inmates were transferred to other institutions, some inmates were placed in the maximum-security block where they were unavailable to us, and we made a few

Table I

Percent of Inmates Who Volunteered for Panel

Inmates	N	Percent of initial group
All inmates solicited	356	-
Completed first questionnaires	170	47.8

Table II

Rate of Continued Participation of Inmates Who Volunteered for Panel

Inmates	N	Percent of initial group
Completed first questionnaire	170	-
Completed first and second questionnaires	150	88.2
Completed all three questionnaires	125	73.5

clerical errors in notifying inmates and arranging schedules. Some inmates were given an unexpectedly early release. For some of our drop-outs, payment had been the original motive for participation, and this motive disappeared when they received money from home or were assigned to paying jobs. Since an inmate who dropped out of the panel would not reappear in a later questionnaire, the effect of the drop-out was magnified. Thus, if the only reasons for not showing up were random problems related to time and place of questionnaire sessions, the sample would show continual shrinkage.

The fact that only 170 out of 356 decided to participate probably indicates that we recruited a relatively willing group of participants, with the noted exceptions. This characteristic, together with the fact that they had "committed" themselves, made it possible for us to make a variety of demands on our participants without incurring a great deal of the sullen hostility with which inmates often express compliance. The foregoing became especially important later on when we were forced to use some time-honored tactics for getting inmates to show up at a given time and place, when they would not do so voluntarily.

The "rotunda" is a central point in the prison through which virtually all inmates pass, at least once each day. A few days before the second questionnaire was to be given, lists were posted in the rotunda, specifying the time at which each inmate was to attend the questionnaire session. The questionnaire sessions were held in the evenings or on Saturday, except for inmates who worked in the evening. A note stated that if an inmate could not attend his assigned session, he should leave a note in our mail box. In those cases we made new assignments.

Inmates who did not show up at their appointed sessions were assigned to a second round of questionnaires. After this second round, we still had a considerable number of drop-outs. We decided to send "lay-in" slips to the remaining non-respondents. A lay-in slip is an official notice requiring, in this case, that the inmate leave his job and report to the rotunda clerk. The clerk then sent him to us. This procedure assured compliance. However, it required that a considerable number of inmates leave their places of work and so required the work supervisors' approval. The supervisor of the furniture factory would not approve of any "lay-ins." Since a sizable percentage of our non-respondents worked in the furniture factory, the supervisor's decision created a substantial loss to us.

At the time of the third questionnaire, we changed our procedure slightly. Rather than post lists, we sent individual notes to the inmates, hoping that this procedure would increase our response rate. Unfortunately, we still got a considerable number of non-respondents. This time, instead of rescheduling the non-respondents, we used the lay-in slips immediately.

At the time of the second and third questionnaires, a certain number of inmates had left the institution's walls to go to one of the other units in the state. (Despite the pain of filling out all those questionnaires, none of our sample escaped!) We administered questionnaires to all who went to the institution's honor farm and made a trip to the other prison in the state and to two of the forest camps, so that we were able to minimize some of those losses. Responses were still lost by transfers, since we could not afford a trip after each questionnaire.

It is instructive to ask how the non-respondents reacted to being forced to show up by the lay-in procedure. When they arrived at the appointed time, the person administering the questionnaire explained why they had been called together. The explanation stated:

1. They had indicated their willingness to complete the study;

2. We could not pay them unless they completed the study;

3. We wanted to "give them a chance" to complete the study.

At one session an inmate said, "I thought you guys said this was voluntary." The response was, "It is; you can leave if you want to. We wanted to get you here and give you a chance to finish and get paid, if you wanted to." In only one case did an inmate decide to leave; he was not the inmate quoted above. A number of inmates, in conversations before the sessions, indicated their irritation with our tactics. Their attitudes can best be expressed in the words, "Well, I'm here so I might as well . . . ." If the non-respondents could be made to show up and if they were allowed to verbally punish us a bit, they were willing to comply and even left with a smile.

The remaining non-respondents had either left the institution or were unavailable to us because of work assignment. How do the various groups of respondents and non-respondents compare in salient characteristics? For the initial group of inmates, who were solicited but did not respond, we, of course, have no attitude data. But two important measures are available. First, we have information on time served. Second, we have information on the number of conduct reports. Table III presents data on the differences in time served by the various groups.

Inmates completing all three questionnaires (group c) had served less time than either the non-volunteers (group a) or the drop-outs (group b). There are a number of ways to explain this finding; attitudes as well as institutional transfers are related to time served. Both factors probably affect participation. Regardless of how the finding is explained, it is important to note that the sample used to analyze change (group c) is biased in the direction of being a relatively short time group in the prison. However, such a statement should be understood as one referring to an "average." In fact, 43 of the inmates in this group had served more than 16 months, and 10 more than 28 months.

Table III

Time Served by Respondent and Non-Respondent Groups
As of September 1, 1962

Group	N	Mean time served in months	p*
(a) Did not volunteer	106	15.41	< .01
(b) Volunteered but did not complete all three questionnaires	44	17.27	< .05
(c) Completed all three questionnaires	125	13.88	

*p = probability of no difference as compared to group c (F test)

Tables IV and V present data on official reports of rule violations. These reports constitute actions by the institution's classification committee and involve some kind of punishment varying from a reprimand to 30 days in solitary confinement. The opportunity to commit rule infractions is obviously a function of time. An inmate who has just arrived in the institution has hardly had time enough to have been caught misbehaving. For this reason, such reports were converted to rates by dividing the number of violations by the number of months served, for each inmate. Unfortunately for statistical purposes, the average inmate in our sample has not had even one rule infraction; thus, he had a rate of zero. Since there are differences in time served by the groups we are comparing, any contrast in rates might be due to the proportion of inmates who have served little time and have accumulated no rule violations. For this reason, we compare separately the proportions having no rule infractions and those having at least one rule infraction.

Table IV*

Percent of Respondent and Non-respondent Groups who Had
No Rule Violations (September 1, 1962)

Group	N	Percent with no rule violations
(a) Did not volunteer	186	50.5
(b) Volunteered but did not complete all questionnaires (drop-outs)	44	50.0
(c) Completed all three questionnaires	125	55.2

*Significant tests were not computed for Tables IV and V because of the skewed slope of the distribution and the comparison techniques, as discussed above.

Table IV shows that group c (those who completed all three questionnaires) include slightly more inmates with no rule infractions. As we have said, this may be due to the time differences between this sample and the other. For group b (the drop-outs), the foregoing appears to be the case. According to Table V, group b has the same mean rate of rule infractions as group c, among those who have rule infractions. On the other hand, the mean rate for group a, the non-volunteers, is considerably higher than that of group c.

One more comparison is instructive. In comparing the drop-outs with those who completed the study, we can avail ourselves of data from the first questionnaire. Table VI compares the two groups on their scores on the major variable to be used in the study, the measure of "protest". Protest, which will be fully explained later on, measures the "set" or "style" the inmate prefers in his relations to staff people. An inmate with a high protest score prefers a tough or aggressive style of relating to staff persons.

Table VI strongly suggests that those who dropped out of the study, after initially agreeing to begin, have more negative attitudes toward the staff. Considering the above differences, it seems reasonable to infer that if we had questionnaire responses from those who did not volunteer, they would turn out to have a higher mean protest score than those who completed the study. It should be noted, again, that the above generalizations merely state a central tendency. Numerous members of the group that completed the questionnaire had high protest scores; conversely, numerous members of the drop-out group had quite low protest scores.

Table V

Mean Rate of Rule Violations per Month among Inmates who had
a Rule Violation, by Respondent and Non-Respondent
Groups (September 1, 1962)

Group	N	Mean rate
(a) Did not volunteer	92	.175
(b) Volunteered but did not complete all questionnaires (drop-outs)	22	.126
(c) Completed all three questionnaires	56	.126

Table VI

Protest Scores of Drop-Outs and Non-Drop-Outs at
Time of First Questionnaire

Group	N	Mean protest score
(b) Volunteered but did not complete all questionnaires	44	29.1
(c) Completed all three questionnaires	125	25.1

Probability of null hypothesis < .01

In summary, there is a series of selection biases which characterize the group that completed all three questionnaires. As compared to the non-respondent groups, those that completed the study were more likely to be short in time served in the prison, were slightly less likely to have at least one rule infraction, had a lower rate of rule infractions, and were likely to have less negative attitudes toward "getting along" with the prison staff. We shall have to consider later how these findings might limit the conclusions that can be drawn from the study.

QUESTIONNAIRE ADMINISTRATION

The questionnaires were administered in group sessions, varying from approximately 5 to 50 inmates. In the larger groups it was common for inmates to sit next to friends, and there was some interaction between inmates. We attempted to curtail interaction by asking that they not discuss their questionnaires, saying that we were anxious to get their own unique, individual response. After explaining the purpose of the study, we briefly explained how to fill out the first page of the questionnaire, which called for factual information, and read and explained the instructions for filling out the first attitude scales. The questionnaire instructions were designed to be self-explanatory, with only one exception--the person-perception instrument used in the second questionnaire. The first and second questionnaires were both handed out in two sections. We included in the second section these parts which would be helped by a special reading and an explanation of the instructions.

THE INSTRUMENTS USED IN THE QUESTIONNAIRE

A relatively large number of instruments were used in the questionnaires. Some we shall describe as they become relevant in the report. The major instruments will be explained in this and the succeeding chapter. The following is a brief listing and resume of the instruments.

Protest: A Likert-type scale, measuring the respondent's preference for a tough or aggressive style of relationship with the staff. The opposite of "protest" is "accommodation."

Sympathy: A Likert-type scale, measuring the inmate's perception of how willing the staff is to share the inmate's point of view.

Reward: A Likert-type scale, measuring the inmate's perception of the specific rewards the staff is willing to provide, whatever their willingness to sympathize with inmates.

Friendship: A measure of the respondent's perceptions about specific members of his friendship group.

Self-type: A series of Likert-type items that were used to classify the respondent as belonging to a "social type" category.

Instrumentalism: A series of contrived situations to which the individual is asked to respond, measuring the willingness of persons to change their protesting or accommodating response to the staff, as the rewards for these alternative response patterns change.

Personalism: A series of contrived situations in which the respondent is asked to guess which, of two choices, probably represents the motivation of the people in the situations.

Work crew status: A procedure used to rate the prestige levels of individual work crews. (Reported in Appendix B.)

<u>Semantic differentials</u>: A series of Osgood-type semantic differentials in which the objects are self, inmates, treatment staff, custody staff. (Reported in Appendix B.)

THE CHARACTERISTICS OF THE INSTRUMENTS

Protest

The protest scale measures the respondent's preferences for a tough or aggressive style of relationship with the staff. It is exemplified by the following items:

1. Inmates should try the soft approach, for a change, in making their wishes known to the staff.

2. It is not a bad thing if the staff gets some trouble from the inmates, every once in a while.

"Protest" is the major variable to be examined in this study, and we will devote Chapter V to a fuller examination of data on its meaning and validity.

Sympathy

The sympathy scale measures the inmate's perception of how willing the staff is to share the inmate's point of view. It consisted of eight items on the first and third questionnaires and five items on the second questionnaire. Typical items are:

1. Most of the correction officers here believe, "Once a con, always a con."

2. Rules here at the Reformatory have been made up with consideration for the the inmates' wishes.

Items for this scale were made up in consultation with members of the staff and other knowledgeable individuals. Some items were taken wholly or partially from scales used by the Youth and Adult Correction Agency of the State of California.[8] Insufficient time was available in advance of the study to test the scale characteristics of the items. Instead, the results of the first administration were subjected to an item analysis with the intention of dropping those items which did not have the correct characteristics. The item analysis was done by the following technique: First we scored the eight items and gave each respondent a scale score. The response format includes the alternatives: strongly agree, mildly agree, neither, mildly disagree, strongly disagree. These responses were given values of 0, 1, 2, 3, and 4, the direction of the values depending on whether the item was chosen to relate to sympathy in a positive or negative direction. The first of the items quoted above is a negative item, the second a positive one. For the first item a "strongly agree" response was given a value of 0; for the second item the same response was given a value of 4. Thus, for eight items we could have had scores ranging from 0 to 32 points; (actually they ranged from 1 to 31).

On the basis of these total scores we selected the highest 25 percent and the lowest 25 percent of the 170 inmates taking the first questionnaire. We then compared the item responses of the two polar groups. A good item, by our criterion, is one in which the high and low groups show highly differentiated response patterns.[9] All items in the scale showed striking differences in the response pattern. Table VII gives examples of the most differentiating item, of the least, and of one somewhere in between in differentiating power. Inspection of Table VII shows that even the least differentiating item, item 8, shows some power to distinguish between high and low groups. Of the high group, only 7, or 15.6 percent, disagreed with the item, whereas of the low group, 20, or 50.0 percent, disagreed with the item. All of the items were retained in the scale.

Reward

The reward scale measures the inmate's perception of specific rewards the staff is willing to provide, whatever their willingness to sympathize with the inmates. It was four items long on the first and third questionnaires and two items long on the second questionnaire. Typical items are:

1. In this institution, the correctional officers will give you a write-up whenever they fell like it, whether there is a good reason or not.

2. If the inmates do just what the staff wants them to do, they get pretty good privileges around here.

This scale was subjected to the same kind of item analysis described in our discussion of the sympathy scale. The items showed similar differentiating properties and all were retained in the scale.

Obviously, the reward and sympathy scales are conceptually rather similar. The question of whether there is any meaningful difference between the two must wait until the data analysis. In analyzing change, reliability problems required a scale of greater length than was provided by either sympathy or reward, and the two were combined into one measure for computing change.

Friendship

This instrument was designed to elicit perceptions of specific friends. The inmate was asked to write down the names of ten friends ("not just your best friends, but the first ten that come to mind"). Then the respondent gave Yes-No answers to a series of questions about characteristics of his ten friends. The items are:

He is a leader among the inmates.

He is not really a criminal.

It makes him sore to have people tell him what to do.

Table VII

Comparison of Responses by High and Low Quartiles on
Sympathy Scale to Three Items

Quartile	Strongly agree	Mildly agree	Neither	Mildly disagree	Strongly disagree
Item 3:					
High......	1	0	2	21	22
Low......	18	10	9	1	2
Item 8:					
High......	12	16	10	4	3
Low......	5	5	10	12	8
Item 5:					
High......	1	5	4	20	15
Low......	15	12	9	4	0

Item 3: Staff members here are not interested in you, but only in your record.
Item 8: To the people on the staff here, you are more than just another case history.
Item 5: The people on the staff here seem to feel that an inmate can never be trusted.

Data taken from first questionnaire.

He is trusted by other inmates.

He is clever in getting what he wants from reformatory officials.

He is a good friend of mine.

He really knows what's going on around here.

I often eat lunch at the same table with him.

This scale was used to categorize the prevailing "social-type" characteristics of the respondent's friends as he perceived them. The four social types that were used are taken from Schrag's analysis of a prison for older offenders.[10] They are:

<u>The square John</u>: This type, the pro-social inmate, retains strong attachments to the outside, legitimate world and is naive about inmate society. He has few loyalties to inmate society.

<u>The con politician:</u> This person is a pseudo-social inmate who has knowledge of

both the inmate and staff worlds and understands how to manipulate each group for his own ends. He often holds a key job in the institution.

<u>The outlaw</u>: This refers to a social inmate who has a minimum of ties to either staff or inmates. He tends toward violence and a harshly exploitive attitude toward others. He is mistrusted by inmates but is in on most of the serious escape plots and riots.

<u>The right guy</u>: This term depicts an anti-social inmate, antagonistic to the values of the legitimate world, but loyal to inmate society. He is a deliberate inmate, unlikely to "squeal," who expresses hatred for the administration but does not typically engage in the aggression toward the administration that characterizes the outlaw.

After consultation with Professor Schrag, an <u>a priori</u> scoring method was developed and is described in Appendix B.

A unique feature of this instrument was that the anonymity of the 10 friends was preserved, so that the inmate was not "ratting" on his friends when he answered our questions.

Self-type

This instrument was used to categorize the inmate as belonging to one or another of the Schrag social types. The instrument consisted of seven self-description items, each allowing a response varying from "strongly agree" to "strongly disagree." Again, in consultation with Professor Schrag a scoring format was designed. For each type, the scoring format prescribed the direction and weight to be given to each item response. For each type, <u>one</u> item was weighted double, as that item had been chosen to uniquely characterize the type. Thus, each respondent had four scores, one for each type. He was coded as belonging to the type corresponding to his highest score, or into one of a number of tied categories. The instrument and scoring format are given in Appendix B.

Instrumentalism

This instrument consists of four contrived situations. Two of them are:

1. Inmates in a reformatory had a lot of serious complaints about working conditions. In one factory, the men were working with poor lighting and ventilation. In fact, it got so hot in the basement of the factory that one man passed out. The work crews have asked several times that something be done to change the conditions. Nothing was done. However, they knew that the factory was under a lot of pressure to get a big order completed and that the last thing the supervisor wanted was any kind of a slowdown. So they threw down their tools and refused to work. They told the supervisor, "We're not going to work until you change things here." How do you personally feel about the inmates' actions?

Strongly agree	Mildly agree	Neither agree nor disagree	Mildly disagree	Strongly disagree
A	a	n	d	D

2. In a prison in the Midwest, the food was pretty bad and the inmates were pretty unhappy about it. The warden told them to quit complaining. The inmates in one cell block began talking about starting some big trouble. If they started trouble, it might do them more harm than good since nobody on the outside seems to care much about what goes on inside this particular prison. However, the inmates decided to start the trouble by plugging up the toilets and flooding out the cell block.

How do you personally feel about the inmates' actions?

(same response format as above)

In the first circumstance, a situation is presented in which the inmates can achieve certain clear gains by engaging in aggressive, or protesting, behavior toward the staff. In the second situation a protesting response is presented as "doing more harm than good." The other two items present situations in which the inmate accommodates to the staff demands. In one, clear gains are presented as arising from the accommodation, but in the other no clear gains are presented. By our definition, an instrumental inmate is one who believes in accommodation when accommodation is effective and believes in protest when protest is effective.

Each response alternative was scored in terms of our conception of an instrumental response. For the first item quoted, if the respondent strongly agreed with the inmates, he was given a score of 4; if he strongly disagreed, he was given a score of 0. On the second item the scoring was reversed; the inmate was given a score of 4 for a "strongly disagree" response. An inmate who chose his response on the basis of the effectiveness of the inmates' strategy, regardless of whether it was protesting or accommodating, would receive 4 points per situation, or 16 points. An inmate who _always_ endorsed the protesting response or _always_ endorsed the accommodating response would receive a score of 8, since he would agree with two of the four items.

Thus we were interested in score variations from 8 to 16. Numerous individuals, it turned out, received scores below 8, indicating that inmates were responding to these stories in terms of some unique qualities of the situation. This suggested that the scale might not be doing the intended job, and variations in the treatment of the scoring were introduced to molify this problem.

Personalism

This instrument was made up of eight to ten items, which were varied somewhat from questionnaire to questionnaire.[11] Typical items are:

1. Inmate Smith runs across some pruno hidden by inmate Vincent.

    He'd like to take a drink of it since he hasn't tasted the stuff in quite a while. Vincent is a leader among the inmates. Smith decides to leave Vincent's pruno alone.

What is your best guess as to why Smith did this?

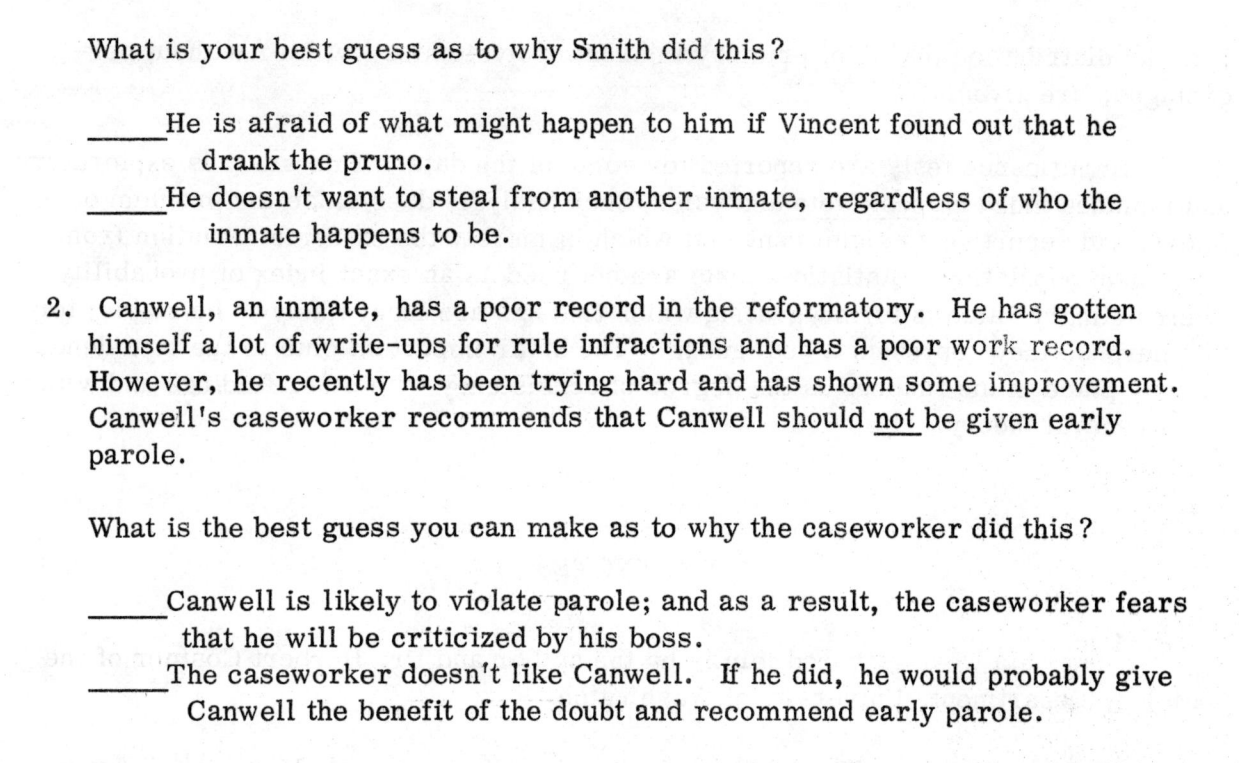

_____ He is afraid of what might happen to him if Vincent found out that he drank the pruno.

_____ He doesn't want to steal from another inmate, regardless of who the inmate happens to be.

2. Canwell, an inmate, has a poor record in the reformatory. He has gotten himself a lot of write-ups for rule infractions and has a poor work record. However, he recently has been trying hard and has shown some improvement. Canwell's caseworker recommends that Canwell should not be given early parole.

What is the best guess you can make as to why the caseworker did this?

_____ Canwell is likely to violate parole; and as a result, the caseworker fears that he will be criticized by his boss.

_____ The caseworker doesn't like Canwell. If he did, he would probably give Canwell the benefit of the doubt and recommend early parole.

Personalism refers to a cognitive state or style. A personalistic actor views the behavior of alter toward ego as a result of particular feelings that alter has developed toward ego. An impersonalistic actor views the behavior of alter as a response to external social pressures. In the first item cited, we scored the first alternative ("He is afraid . . . .") as a personalistic response, and in the second item we scored the second alternative ("He doesn't like . . . .") as a personalistic response. The rest of the scoring can be found in Appendix B.

The personalism scale was subjected to the same kind of item analysis as were the sympathy and reward scales. The results were somewhat disappointing as compared to the other scales. Although all items discriminated in the appropriate direction, some of the differences between high and low groups were rather weak. For this reason, a total personalism score was computed by summing the scores taken from each of the three questionnaires. It was hoped that the greater length of the scale would add to its reliability and increase its usefulness for analyzing change in protest over the time span of the study.

STATISTICAL TECHNIQUES USED IN THE STUDY

Many of the variables in the present study are continuous and can be adapted to the use of means. By establishing multiple cutting points, i.e., polyotomies, such as the quartiles that were given in the present chapter, percentage distributions can be given. There are advantages and disadvantages to the use of percentages. It was felt that the mean would give more stable, consistent findings because of its highly efficient sampling distribution,[12] and the problem of setting points for a polyotomy. Polyotomies, of course, give a picture of the variability of the distribution. When it is the distribution that is of primary interest, polyotomies, with or without percentages, are given.

Significance tests are reported for some of the data. This study is exploratory and includes much ex post facto analysis. Such analysis does raise the problem of finding and reporting as significant that which is merely the extreme variation from a common population. Statistical tests are not used as an exact index of probability. Their primary value is for suggesting which findings are most likely to be stable; for this purpose they represent a best guess. The other important clue to the confidence we may place in the findings is the degree of consistency with other findings and with some general theory.

FOOTNOTES

[1] The data were gathered jointly by the author and Dr. Herbert Costner of the Sociology Department, University of Washington.

[2] Stanton Wheeler, "Social Organization in a Correctional Community" (unpublished Ph.D. dissertation, University of Washington, Seattle, 1958).

[3] Department of Institutions, State of Washington, Research Review, No. VIII, 1962, Table V.

[4] Ibid., Tables V and VI.

[5] Richard McCleery, "The Governmental Process and Informal Social Control" in Donald R. Cressey (ed.), The Prison (New York: Holt, Rinehart and Winston, 1961).

[6] Richard A. Cloward, "Social Control in the Prison" in George H. Grosser (ed.), Theoretical Studies in the Social Organization of the Prison (New York: Social Science Research Council, Pamphlet No. 15, 1960).

[7] Stanton Wheeler, "Socialization in Correctional Communities," American Sociological Review, XXVI (October, 1961), 699-712; Daniel Glaser and John R. Stratton, "Measuring Change in Prison" in Donald R. Cressey (ed.), The Prison (New York: Holt, Rinehart, and Winston, 1961), Chapter 10; Peter G. Garabedian, "Social Roles and the Process of Socialization in a Prison Community," Social Problems, XI: 2 (Fall, 1963), 139-152.

[8] Some of these items are in Alfred Himelson and Paul Takagi, Research Report No. 7, Research Division, Department of Corrections, Youth and Adult Corrections Agency, State of California.

[9] Allen L. Edwards, Techniques of Attitude Scale Construction (New York: Appleton-Century-Crofts, Inc., 1957), pp. 152-156.

[10] Clarence C. Schrag, "Social Types in a Prison Community" (unpublished Master's thesis, University of Washington, Seattle, 1944). The description of the types are condensed from Chapters 5, 6, 7, and 8.

[11] This variable was used for testing a series of notions about the effects of various kinds of information on status threat.

[12] Hubert M. Blalock, Social Statistics (New York: McGraw-Hill Book Co., 1960), p. 157.

CHAPTER V

THE MEANING OF PROTEST

THE RELATIONSHIP BETWEEN CONFLICT AND PROTEST

Earlier we offered a definition of the term "conflict." It contained at least four important elements:

<u>Awareness</u>: The parties to a conflict are aware that they are behaving in ways contrary to the wishes of the other.

<u>Variety</u>: The parties persistently behave in a variety of different ways that are contrary to the wishes of the other and upsetting to the dominance relations between the parties. Differences over minor situations as well as over major issues involving crucial norms characterize conflict behavior.

<u>Interaction</u>: Conflict involves the behavior of two or more parties, not the acts of a single individual to which others do not respond.

<u>Behavior</u>: Conflict refers to predispositions that are expressed as behavior, not to feeling states that remain hidden.

The present study does not involve observing interactions between staff and inmates. Our major dependent variable is protest, using a verbal scale as a measure. Furthermore, the scale was given to inmates only, not to staff members. For these reasons we shall devote the present chapter to asking in what way our protest measure serves as an <u>index</u> to conflict relations, as exemplified in the above four elements. What is the meaning of protest?

DEVELOPMENT OF THE SCALE

"Protest" has been previously defined as a measure of the inmate's preference for a tough or aggressive style of interaction with staff members. Does he prefer to make trouble--disobey orders, refuse to follow routines, speak offensively--or does he prefer to "go along" and <u>accommodate</u> his wishes to those of the staff? A series of scale items was developed in consultation with knowledgeable persons on the staff of the institution and elsewhere. Items were also drawn, typically in modified form, from scales used by the Youth and Adult Correction Agency of the State of California.[1] The scale was 15 items in length on the first and third questionnaires and 6 items in length on the second questionnaire. The initial version read as follows:

1. Needs of the inmates are often ignored because the staff can buy off a few inmate leaders and "to hell with the rest."

2. An inmate should usually try to "go along" with what the staff wants.

3. When a riot starts in a prison, it is usually because the inmates have been pushed too far.

4. Inmates ought to try soft-pedaling some of their complaints and try saying a few nice things to the staff once in a while.

5. Riots are the worst things that can happen in a prison.

6. The trouble with most inmates is that they have a bad attitude against the staff.

7. The inmates in this place don't stick up for their rights.

8. Inmates should try the soft approach, for a change, in making their wishes known to the staff.

9. I feel pretty strong about some of the complaints we inmates have.

10. When a big inmate blow-up starts in a prison, it is usually justified.

11. In prison, it is sometimes necessary to ignore what you think is right and "give in" a little, in order to avoid trouble and arguments with the staff.

12. I don't mind hurrying along when I'm doing something if its' necessary in order to make the institutional time schedule run O.K.

13. It's not a bad thing if the staff gets some trouble from the inmates every once in a while.

14. One thing I don't like to do is address all the officers as "Mister."

15. There is no good reason to be different when visitors are around, even if the staff wants us to.

These protest scales were subjected to the same kind of item analysis as were the sympathy, reward, and personalism scales. Excellent results were produced by the analysis. All of the items discriminated in the appropriate direction; most of them showed a striking degree of discrimination. Table VIII shows the response

Table VIII

Comparison of Responses by High and Low Quartiles on
Protest Scale to Three Items

Quartile	Strongly agree	Mildly agree	Neither	Mildly disagree	Strongly disagree
Item 14:					
High......	24	15	4	2	0
Low......	4	3	4	15	17
Item 11:					
High......	21	13	2	3	6
Low......	29	12	0	0	3
Item 13:					
High......	9	18	12	5	1
Low......	3	4	7	13	17

Item 14: One thing I don't like to do is address all officers as "Mister."
Item 11: In prison, it is sometimes necessary to ignore what you think is right and "give in" a little in order to avoid trouble and arguments with the staff.
Item 13: It's not a bad thing if the staff gets some trouble from the inmates every once in a while.

Data taken from first questionnaire.

patterns of the highest and lowest quartiles on the protest scale. The first item (item 14) is the most discriminating, the second item (item 11) is the least discriminating, and the last item (item 13) falls somewhere in the middle of the range. The item analysis suggested that the wording of item 11 be changed. Apparently, protesting inmates tend to picture themselves as _sometimes_ doing a good deal of "giving in." As worded, the question becomes one which asks something about the _reality_ situation, as the inmate perceives it. On subsequent questionnaires, the wording was changed to read, "In prison, it is sometimes a good idea to 'give in' a little to avoid trouble and arguments with the staff." The rewording emphasized that giving in was a "good idea," rather than something one was forced to do. The new version substantially improved the response characteristics of the question. The foregoing may suggest that protest is a measure of the inmate's _preference_ for compliance and not the "objective" degree of compliance. His preference may _structure_ but not _determine_ his behavior.

The relative case with which we were able to construct a scale to measure protest suggested that it was a relatively simple concept and might have a unidimensional structure.

THE CHARACTERISTICS OF SELECTED ITEMS

There are two different types of items in the protest scales. The first type consists of items that refer to rather specific situations: keeping the time schedule running, how to behave with visitors around, riots, etc. The second type is the item that refers to staff-inmate relations in quite general terms: inmates don't stand up for their rights, the soft approach is needed, trouble is not a bad thing, etc. The second type of item, the general type, had rather uniform response characteristics. If the item was positively related to protest, the high quartile group would tend to agree with it, and the low-quartile group would tend to disagree with it. On the type of item that referred to specific situations, quite a different pattern emerged. On most of these items the quartile groups tended to endorse the item in the same direction, sometimes in a protesting direction, sometimes in an accommodating direction. (Nonetheless, there are differences in the degree of endorsement by the two different groups.)

Item 12 in Table IX illustrates the above comments. The overwhelming majority of accommodating inmates, 38 out of 42, agrees with the item. However, a virtual majority of protesting inmates also agrees with the item, 22 out of 45. Only 12 of the 45 protesting inmates disagree with the item. Apparently there is some agreement between inmates that the time schedule requires conformity. Looking at some other items, we find that 15 of the 45 protestors agree with riots are the worst things that can happen in a prison, and 17 of the protestors disagree that there is no reason to behave differently when visitors are around.

The foregoing suggests that as we tie our measure of protest to concrete circumstances, situation-specific attitudes begin to take over. There may be some need to accommodate to certain key staff demands, such as those relating to visitors and time schedules. And riots may indeed be pretty nasty affairs, even to those inmates who are quite willing to behave in a hostile manner toward the staff.

Only one "specific" item distinguishes between protestors and accommodators in the same way as the "general" items. Almost all protestors agree that they don't like to call officers "Mister," and almost all accommodators disagree with that item. Why is this item not contaminated by the situation-specific attitudes we inferred from the other items? Probably three features of this item account for the response pattern. First, the staff of this institution does not demand this form of deference, although it is preferred. Inmates who avoid calling officers "Mister" do so by avoiding the use of names or by some other subterfuge. Second, the act may have a well-understood character in the symbolic structure of prison life. The item refers to an act that may have one, and only one, meaning, and that is as a sign of deference toward the staff. On the other hand, one's avoidance of riot situations can be interpreted either as being an indicator of "prison wisdom" or as a desire to comply with the staff. Third, a theoretical point is relevant. We hypothesized earlier that the greater the concern with the dominance-submission dimension, the more likely is conflict to occur. The clear-cut deference meaning of this item may make compliance difficult for an inmate who is characterized by a primary concern with relative dominance, even if he imagines that this item represents a key staff demand. Since protestors show a very strong tendency

Table IX

Comparison of Responses by High and Low Quartiles on Protest
Scale to Five "Specific" Items

Quartile	Strongly agree	Mildly agree	Neither	Mildly disagree	Strongly disagree
Item 3:					
High	29	10	0	4	2
Low	8	3	9	12	12
Item 5:					
High	11	4	3	7	20
Low	22	10	4	5	3
Item 12:					
High	5	17	11	8	4
Low	27	11	3		1
Item 14:					
High	24	15	4	2	0
Low	4	3	4	15	17
Item 15:					
High	15	7	6	8	9
Low	6	3	7	7	21

Item 3: When a riot starts in prison, it is usually because the inmates have been pushed too far.
Item 5: Riots are the worst things that can happen in a prison.
Item 12: I don't mind hurrying if it is necessary to make the institutional time schedule run OK.
Item 14: One thing I don't like to do is address all officers as "Mister."
Item 15: There is no reason to behave differently when visitors are around, even if the staff wants us to.

Data taken from first questionnaire.

not to comply on this item, we are given a bit of confirmation for the earlier hypothesis.

Our analysis of the items referring to specific behaviors suggests that they are relatively poor indicators of protest. The exception to this rule may occur where the act has a clear meaning as a symbol of dominance and when the inmate is not coerced into compliance. Does the foregoing indicate that protest is a state of mind of the inmate, unrelated to his behavior or interaction with the staff? Not necessarily. While an officer may not immediately respond to a non-deferential inmate, a later violation of the institution's rules may find this officer anxious to punish the inmate. And, of course, the deferential inmate may find a warm spot in the officer's heart.

PROTEST AND ITS OBJECTS

Conflict is a relationships between parties. What are the attitudes of the protesting inmates toward different categories of persons in the prison? A semantic differential was used in our questionnaire, in which the inmate was asked to rate various objects using a series of 18 pairs of words. For the sake of simplicity we shall use the single word-pair, "I like - I dislike," to illustrate. The ratings were on a 7-point scale, where 7 is the maximum endorsement of the phrase, "I dislike." Let us compare the ratings by the high and low-protest quartiles of the objects: custody staff, treatment staff, and inmates.

Numerous qualities of protest are suggested by Table X. Protestors are considerably more hostile toward custody staff than are accommodators--a difference of 2.29 points on a 7-point scale. The same relationship is found in attitudes toward treatment staff. However, in the case of attitudes toward treatment staff, the difference between the quartiles is smaller--1.45 points. Furthermore, both protestors and accommodators are less hostile toward treatment staff than toward custody staff. These findings are in contrast with those of Wheeler, who found that inmates did not differentiate much between custody and treatment staff in their perception of staff attitudes.[2]

The comparison of ratings also suggests that protest bears little relation to attitudes toward inmates. Again, this finding is in contrast to those of Wheeler, if the opposite of protest is equated with Wheeler's measure of conformity toward staff expectations.[3] We shall take up this question shortly.

In conclusion, the above semantic differential ratings suggest that protest is most clearly tied to attitudes toward custody staff. In a prison custodial officers are the most direct, face-to-face agents of official authority. Furthermore, the permissive attitudes of the treatment staff may mean that an inmate who behaves in a hostile manner is more likely to be censured by custody staff than by treatment staff. The fact that protest correlates more highly with attitudes toward custody staff than it does with attitudes toward treatment staff seems to indicate that the protestor is more highly involved in conflict with custody persons than he is with treatment persons.

PROTEST AND VIOLATION OF INSTITUTIONAL RULES

Although we have indicated that protest may not relate to any specific instance of non-compliant behavior, it is important to know whether or not it does relate to

Table X

Semantic Differential Ratings of Custody Staff, Treatment Staff,
and Inmates by Protest Quartiles

Object	Protest quartile	Mean rating (7 = "I dislike")	Difference between quartiles
Custody staff	High	5.64	2.29
	Low	3.35	
Treatment staff	High	3.82	1.45
	Low	2.37	
Inmates	High	4.00	.19
	Low	4.19	

Data taken from first questionnaire.

non-compliance in general. One way to find out is to ask for self-reports. We asked inmates to respond to the item, "One thing I won't do is address all the officers as 'Mister,'" and to the item, "If I don't like my food, I'll throw it on the floor." The latter item refers to a practice sometimes observed in prison mess halls. Both items refer to violations of institutional regulations.

The item about calling officers "Mister" correlated quite highly with protest. The second item produced an unusual response pattern. No accommodators agreed with it, and only 5 out of 45 protestors agreed with the item, although considerably more accommodators *strongly* disagreed than did protestors. Anyone who has been in a prison mess hall can testify to the discrepancy between these self-reports and actual behavior. We wondered if the wording of the question suggested childlike behavior. We wondered if the wording of the question suggested childlike behavior. The question was reworded to sound like a simple report of behavior, rather than a report of temper tantrum ("I often throw food on the mess hall floor"). The same response pattern appeared. Two alternative conclusions are suggested by these findings. First, it may be that inmates were unwilling to report on actual incidents of behavior that were a clear violation of important institutional rules. Apparently our promise of confidentiality had been taken seriously, because inmates endorsed very antagonistic items on other portions of the questionnaire. When it came to admitting misbehavior, they may not have been willing to take a chance--not unreasonable decision. The second possibility that is suggested by the data on self-reported behavior is that the inmates may be making quite accurate reports of their own performance, as that behavior is perceived by the occupants of the prison world. When an inmate clearly and visibly throws food on the floor, he is likely to be reported or "tagged" by an officer. Thus, unless he is especially angry, he is likely to "flick" or "drop" the food on the floor, out of sight of the officers. In other words, behavior has a situation-specific character that goes beyond a simple description. Neither the inmate nor the guard look at _what_ was done; rather, they look at _how_ the behavior was enacted. If the behavior was not clearly visible, or if it appeared to be accidental (and if the rule violation was committed by a well-mannered inmate it is likely to be seen as accidental), the behavior doesn't "count." Nonetheless, a large quantity of food ends up on the floor.

A second way of measuring rule-violating behavior is to look at the institution records. The nature of the data was described, briefly, in the preceding chapter. The list of possible rule violations is a long one, but the most typical offenses are insubordination, having contraband, cursing an officer, fighting, or refusing to work. When an inmate is found committing one of these offenses, a number of alternatives are possible. The offense may be ignored, possibly being considered trivial. The officer may decide to handle it by himself. Officers are loathe to issue too many formal "write-ups" for fear that they will be seen as lacking control over the inmates in their charge. If the write-up is issued, the Captain of Guards or perhaps the caseworker may handle the matter by "counseling" or some informal punishment. If it is too serious a violation to be dealt with informally, if it is repeated, or if for any other reason the staff wishes to, the inmate is sent before the adjustment committee. Then a formal charge is lodged and the inmate may be placed in a "holding cell" in the maximum-security cell block until disposition of the case. All cases in which the inmate is adjudged guilty by the adjustment committee (and almost all cases are adjudged guilty) are recorded in the inmate's classification file.

We had access to the highly selected data in the classification file. Like all official judicial data, these are highly weighted with the serious, persistent violators rather than the occasional, non-serious violator, although it is the latter that constitutes the bulk of violations. The data from these files were coded into two categories --assault and other rule violations. Table XI shows the relationship of rule infractions to the protest quartiles. As was earlier mentioned, we computed rates, but for clarity we shall simply look at the percentage having one or more rule infractions.

Table XI shows that the proportion having one or more rule infractions was approximately twice as high in the highest protest quartile as compared to the lowest. It also shows that not all protestors have had rule infractions, nor have all accommodators avoided rule infractions. The exceptions might be explained by noting time as a factor. Many inmates in our study have not been around long enough to get into too much trouble, even though their protest level might predispose them in that direction. On the other hand, our records go back to the beginning of the inmate's sentence. His current attitudes might preclude getting in trouble, but his former escapades are still recorded.

In summary, self-reports of rule-violating behavior do not relate very clearly to protest. Conversely, institutional reports of violations are strongly related to protest. If we take the institutional record as the best index, the most effective way to find out if the individual engages in rule violations is <u>not to ask him what he does but rather to ask him what his preferences for misbehavior are.</u> Our protest scale appears to be an index of involvement in serious, persistent misbehavior patterns.

Table XI

Relationship Between Protest and Rule Infractions*

Protest quartile	Percent having one or more rule infractions**	N
Highest	67	45
Medium high	49	36
Medium low	39	46
Lowest	33	43

*Rule infractions as of September 1, 1962.

**Excluding assault against another inmate.

Data on protest scores taken from first questionnaire.

The institutional recoreds, themselves, could be used as such an index. But, for analyzing individual differences and observing change, such records are much too insensitive. Most individuals do not have a rule infraction, and relatively few received a new infraction over the course of the study. Thus, protest combines sensitivity with a high relationship to the interaction pattern to which it is supposed to be related.

CONFORMITY TO STAFF EXPECTATIONS AND RULE VIOLATIONS

In Chapter I we reported on Wheeler's use of an index of conformity to staff rule expectations. The index consisted of a series of contrived situations regarding inmate behavior. In our second questionnaire we used two of Wheeler's items. They are reproduced in Appendix B. One refers to an inmate defending an officer's action; the other involves an inmate clearing himself of an escape charge by telling the name of the inmates who were involved. In both of the items there is a clear inmate expectation which is opposite to the staff expectations as Wheeler found them. Wheeler's items are an index to the identification of the inmate with other inmates, while the protest scale may be viewed as an index of the amount of conflict with the staff.

Table XII shows the relation of an index constructed from these two items to recorded rule violations. A range of 0 to 6 was obtained by combining the two items. To break the scale into approximate quartiles, the end categories were combined.

Table XII shows that those high in inmate conformity have a greater tendency to have rule violations than those low in inmate conformity. But the relationship shows considerably less strength than does the relationship of rule violations to protest. We therefore conclude that protest is a better index to a pattern of generalized

Table XII

Relationship Between Conformity to Inmate Role Expectations
and Rule Violations*

Score (High = 6)	Percent having one or more rule infractions**	N
0-2	41	29
3	32	40
4	46	39
5-6	51	37

*Rule infraction data as of September 1, 1962.

**Excluding assault against another inmate.

Data on conformity scores taken from second questionnaire.

non-compliant behavior than is Wheeler's measure of conformity to inmate norms. This conclusion needs to be tentative, however, as our adaptation of Wheeler's scale includes only two of his five items.

PROTEST AND INMATE ASSAULT

Table XIII shows the relationship between assault against another inmate and level of protest. No consistent pattern appears in Table XIII. As was suggested in our earlier discussion of the objects of protest, high protest connotes neither a hostile nor a friendly relationship to other inmates.

PROTEST AND CONFLICT: A SUMMARY

At the beginning of this chapter we laid down four elements of our definition of conflict: awareness, variety, interaction, and behavior. The development and analysis of the scale shows that the protest measure includes all of these elements.

Individuals who endorse this scale are not merely indicating that they engage in some specific behavior; in effect they say, "I am willing to give the staff some trouble." They are aware of this tendency to behave contrary to staff wishes. In fact, items which are specific do not correlate well with the scale; perhaps an individual can endorse such items in a protesting direction without <u>seeing himself</u> as being troublesome to the staff or vice versa.

Table XIII

Relationship Between Assault Against Another
Inmate and Protest

Protest quartile	Percent having rule infraction for inmate assault*	N
Highest	4	45
Medium high	8	36
Medium low	4	46
Lowest	12	43

*Rule infraction data as of September 1, 1962.

Data on protest scores from first questionnaire.

The variety that is characteristic of conflict was created by the wording of the questions. Institutional records of rule infractions serve as an index to persistent misbehavior, and correlation of those recorded infractions with protest suggests that our scale measures a persistent, rather than an occasional, phenomenon.

Is the protest scale a measure of behavior? It is probably a relatively poor predictor of any specific act. Rather, it is an index of a behavior syndrome. We considered using self-reports of behavior. However, such reports lack the element of awareness. An individual may misbehave without seeing himself as so doing. In addition, self-reports may lack variety. The individual's protest score has greater verity, it seems, as an index of persistent misbehavior.

We also suggest that, to the extent that protest is related to a variety of persistent misbehaviors, misbehavior which is responded to by the staff, it is an index to the type of interaction that exists between the staff members and the inmate. Probably the reason protest relates so well to such a selective index of behavior as recorded rule infractions is that it connotes a state of mind, a style of response, which is irritating to the staff and which is likely to bring swift punishment when the individual engaged in a specific act of misbehavior.

Finally, we found that protest related more highly to negative attitudes toward custody staff, as compared to treatment staff. It is likely that protest indicates a relationship to custody staff more clearly than to treatment staff.

FOOTNOTES

[1] Some of these items are in Alfred Himelson and Paul Takagi, *Research Report No. 7*, Research Division, Department of Corrections, Youth and Adult Corrections Agency, State of California.

[2] Stanton Wheeler, "Role Conflict in Correctional Communities" in Donald Cressey (ed.), *The Prison* (New York: Holt, Rinehart, and Winston, 1961), p. 244.

[3] Stanton Wheeler, "Social Organization in a Correctional Community" (unpublished Ph.D. dissertation, University of Washington, Seattle, 1958). For example, Wheeler shows that conformity to staff role expectations is related to extensiveness to primary group ties to inmates. See p. 109.

CHAPTER VI

THE COGNITIVE WORLD OF THE PROTESTOR

In the material in the present chapter and in Chapter VII we shall look at relationships between static variables--variables measured at some instant in time. In Chapter VII we shall make a few inferences as to longitudinal change by comparing inmates who had spent different amounts of time in the Reformatory, exposed in greater or lesser degree to certain stimuli. Chapter VIII will be concerned with dynamic or longitudinal measures--with changes in the level of the variables over the time period of the panel.

The present chapter will consider the interrelationships between those phenomena that sociologists are accustomed to call "social-psychological." The concern here will be with the existence of patterns of cognition and self-conception. How do our findings relate to the conflict theory outlined above, and what suggestions arise from the data analysis to suggest elaborations or reformulations of the theory?

EXCHANGE BALANCE AND PROTEST

In Chapter II it was argued that one of the determinants of status is the nature of the exchange of values that takes place between staff and inmate. Hypothesis 5 stated:

An unbalanced exchange relationship is a symbol of the dominance of the favored party.

Phrased in terms of cognition, Hypothesis 5 states:

A person who sees himself as giving more compliance to the staff than the values he receives in return will experience status threat.

In Chapter II we discussed two kinds of returns the staff may offer. First, the staff may offer specific privileges: parole recommendations, good jobs, more liberal custody status, school, etc. Second, the staff member may offer a sympathetic response to the inmate. The staff may change its view of the inmate's character. They may come to perceive the inmate as trustworthy, intelligent, important, etc. The first kind of value was incorporated in the reward scale, while the second kind of value was incorporated in the sympathy scale. When a staff member gives an inmate specific institutional privileges, the cost to himself is often very little. On the other hand, offering sympathy may represent a very large investment. It is an investment of the staff member's own personality into the relationship. We hypothesize that:

1. The sympathy and reward scales will correlate negatively with the protest scale.

2. "Sympathy" is a greater value than institutional privilege. Thus, the correlation of the sympathy scale with the protest scale will be higher than the correlation of the reward scale with the protest scale.

Figure 1 presents the intercorrelations among the protest, sympathy, and reward scale. As hypothesized, the sympathy and reward scales correlate highly with protest. The protesting inmate perceives the staff as highly unsympathetic and as offering few privileges, whereas the accommodating inmate perceives the staff as highly sympathetic and offering many privileges.

Figure 1

Intercorrelation Matrix of Protest, Sympathy, and Reward

	Protest	Sympathy	Reward
Protest			
Sympathy	-.61		
Reward	-.52	.64	

N = 170
For the correlations above, the hypothesis that the population r is zero is rejected, $p < .01$.

Data taken from first questionnaire

The protest scale correlates <u>most</u> highly with the sympathy scale, as hypothesized. However, the reward scale contains only half as many items (four) as the sympathy scale and therefore is more likely to be unreliable. Since the unreliability of a scale normally reduces its correlations with other scales, the possibly low reliability of the reward scale may explain the lower correlation between protest and reward. The second hypothesis above cannot be considered adequately confirmed as yet. The highest correlation in Figure 1 is between reward and sympathy. This suggests that they may not be empirically separable, even if they are logically different. One item in the reward scale is, "In this institution, the correctional officers will give you a write-up whenever they feel like it, whether they feel like it, whether there is a good reason or not." It was included on the assumption that officers may be

In summary, the protestor is found to perceive the staff as unsympathetic toward inmates. A key part of this image is the perception that staff members will not change their view of inmates. Furthermore, the protestor sees the staff as unjust; a correctional officer is likely to institute formal punishment against an inmate without a good reason. In general, the protestor sees little that can be offered him in exchange for conformity. He is unlikely to see the "rehabilitation program" as useful, though here he may have a more favorable perception than in other areas. The accommodator, conversely, sees the staff as sympathetic, or willing to change its view of the inmate, as relatively just, and as offering much that is useful in the way of rehabilitation. This offers tentative support for our theoretical statement about the effects of an unfavorable exchange of values.

THE PERSONAL QUALITIES OF STAFF AND INMATES AND PROTEST

A semantic differential[1] was administered to our respondents using 18 word pairs and the objects, "inmate" and "custody staff," among others.[2] A profile of the responses is presented in Figure 2, using only those word pairs where there was a substantial difference between the perceptions of custody staff and of inmates. Table XV shows the mean scores for each of the groups.

A look at Figure 2 shows some interesting differences in perception. In general, the differences between the protestors and accommodators are small on perception of inmates and larger on perception of custody staff. The largest difference between perceptions of inmates is on the word pair, "important - unimportant." Protestors see inmates as less important than do accommodators. Again this suggests the concern of the protestors with the dimension of status or dominance.

The largest difference in perception of custody staff is on the word pair, "fair - unfair." Protestors are far more likely to perceive staff as highly unfair than are accommodators.

The next largest difference in perception of custody staff is "important - unimportant," with protestors seeing the staff as less important than do the accommodators. The clearest images that relate to protest are as follows, stated in order of the magnitude of the differences: Protestors see the staff as unfair, unimportant, unstable, dull, and different from themselves. It is difficult to guess at the particular meaning of the appallation "unstable" to the protestors, but is is, at least, a good guess that it is an accusation of injustice -- custody staff can't be counted on to keep promises.

Figure 2 shows that inmates tend to rate guards higher than inmates on a number of evaluative word pairs. For accommodators, guards are perceived as more fair than inmates, more stable, stronger, more important, and wiser. Even for protestors, perceptions of guards are about as favorable as inmates on "stability," "importance," and "wisdom." <u>For the overall inmate group, inmates are perceived in a less favorable fashion than are guards on the majority of evaluative items.</u>

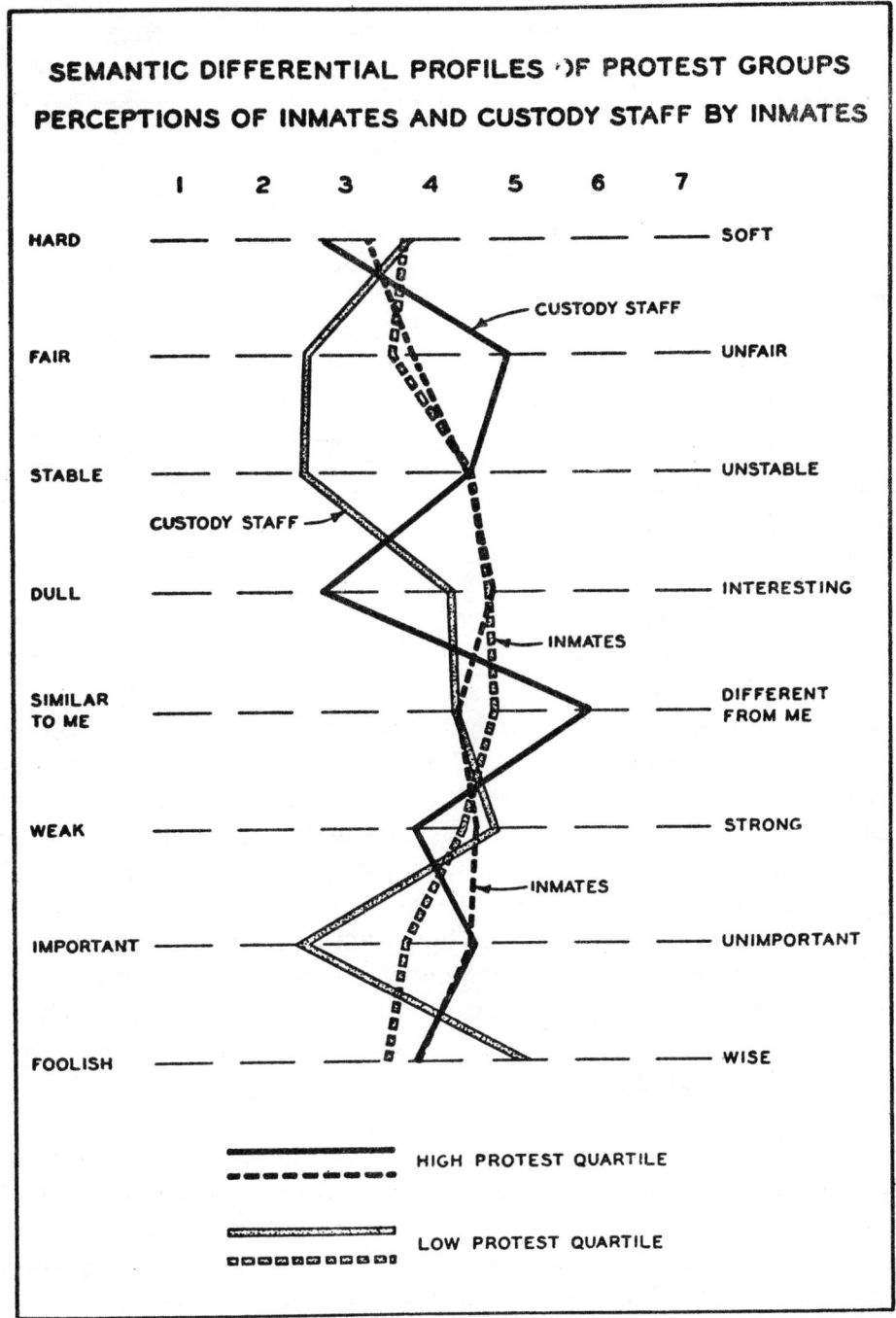

FIGURE 2

Table XV

Mean Scores of Protest Quartiles on Semantic Differential

Word pair	Inmates High quartile	Inmates Low quartile	Custody Staff High quartile	Custody Staff Low quartile
Hard - soft	3.25	3.67	2.66	3.72
Fair - unfair	3.73	3.53	4.89	2.51
Stable - unstable	4.39	4.46	4.45	2.47
Dull - interesting	4.70	4.65	2.66	4.24
Similar to me - different from me	4.31	4.74	5.87	4.30
Weak - strong	4.50	4.37	3.75	4.72
Important - unimportant	4.41	3.65	4.48	2.44
Foolish - wise	3.79	3.44	3.77	5.09

Strongest endorsement of right-hand word = 7
Strongest endorsement of left-hand word = 1

Data taken from first questionnaire.

Several items that we have looked at thus far provide some evidence about another theoretical point made in Chapter III. We suggested that conflict with the staff heightens the inmate's sense of identification with other inmates. Four items suggest identification. Three of them from the semantic differential are: "liking," "similar to me," and "interesting." The fourth item is from the sympathy scale, i.e., ". . . the only persons you can really talk your problems over with are your friends among your fellow inmates." The last item particularly suggests the heightened sense of social equality that was hypothesized to characterize conflict-oriented inmates in Chapter III. While the protestors did not express more "liking" than did the accommodators, the other three items did correlate with protest. The item about "talking things over" correlated very highly with protest.

Protestors do not like inmates any more than do accommodators. But, as anticipated, they feel considerable "oneness" with other inmates; the word often used for this state is "sympatico." Interestingly, this identification does not preclude having negative perceptions about inmates, and in the case of the word pair, "important - unimportant," protest appears to enhance the negative perception.

PERSONALISM AND PROTEST

It was argued earlier that the effect of an exchange imbalance would be diminished if the inmate did not perceive demands made upon him as arising from the wishes of the person who enforced those demands. If, instead, the inmate perceives that the demands arise from the situation faced by the other, he is less likely to see compliance as an act of negotiation with a _person_. Acts of negotiation have a dominance meaning, and therefore such an inmate is less likely to be a protestor than one who holds a personal view of the situation.

According to McCleery, authoritarian control does not rest on the use of punitive sanctions but on the formulation of _definitions of the situation_ and the communication of these definitions throughout the system.[3] The major way in which this is done is by the use of signed orders and personal commands. This is somewhat confusing in the light of McCleery's own statement that the "autocrat of militant penal bureaucracy will confess an inability to initiate changes in routine."[4] In the prison, as in other administrative systems, it is important that commands do _not_ have a personal character. Personal commands are less likely to induce compliance than commands that have an impersonal source in some rational requirement or in some "traditional way of doing things." Prisons and other similar organizations resist change in routine because a change raises the spectre of personal demands. Consequently, signed orders and personal commands are rarely issued by persons who enforce them. Instead, orders are issued by some higher authority. Gouldner refers to this phenomenon as the "screening function" of bureaucratic rules.[5] Bureaucratic rules, among other things, reduce the stigma that might inhere in personal compliance. In the perfect model of a bureaucracy, from this point of view, no one ever acts on his own authority. Weber's emphasis on the role of expertise in bureaucracy gives us another example of the depersonalization of commands.[6] An expert does not act out of personal will but out of knowledge of a rational set of principles. It is not _he_ who commands; his commands stem from the rational knowledge of which he is only an interpreter.

There are a number of ways of testing the hypothesis about the effect on protest of depersonalization of relationships. First, one might interview the inmate in detail about his knowledge of the motivation of others in the institution. Alternatively, one might administer an "objective" test covering the same sort of thing. To be able to generalize a causal sequence, showing the relation between interpersonal interaction and personalism, would require that uniform kinds of interactions occur repetitively, with uniform motivations, and that these interactions be relatively crucial to the individual. There are great analytic difficulties involved in ascertaining such processes, and it might well prove fruitless to try to do so.

Another way of testing the hypothesis about depersonalization is by assuming that certain positions in the formal system of the prison give the inmate better insight into the impersonal sources of actions. For example, the role of the clerk who works closely with staff members might be such a position. However, any specific hypotheses about the relation of formal position to impersonalism seem premature. It is also reasonable to suppose that the inmate clerk has insight into the highly personalistic motivations that affect staff members--we are not arguing that the sources of action are really impersonal. It would be difficult to hypothesize what formal positions would produce an impersonalistic outlook.

Instead of rooting impersonalism to formal position or to personal experience, it is possible to argue that impersonalism can also be hypothesized to be a general cognitive state. It may be that some individuals have an impersonalistic perspective on a wide variety of interactions that they experience, whether the interactions relate to authority or to interpersonal experience. The personalism scale describe in Chapter IV was developed to measure this tendency. A high personalism score connotes a tendency to see demands as arising from the wishes and attitudes of the other. A low personalism score connotes an individual who sees a situational origin to demands. On the assumption that a general cognitive state was being measured, the scale was not restricted to interpersonal demands, but was related to any kinds of interactions that might occur. A personalistic inmate perceives acts of generosity as having a personal rather than a situational origin; he argues that when an officer behaves in a non-punitive fashion toward an inmate, he does so out of friendship rather than professional concern. He also argues that when individuals conform to interpersonal demands they do so as a result of specific attitudes toward the person making the demands, rather than as a result of broad situational pressures. If the personalism "state" is found to be related to the level of protest, then we can tentatively extrapolate to the effects of specific interactions that have personalistic bases. The hypothesis about personalism can be stated as follows:

> Personalistic inmates tend to see the acts of staff members as acts of will and therefore assertions as to staff dominance. Personalistic inmates therefore may be expected to score higher on protest than impersonalistic inmates.

This hypothesis was not substantiated by the static data for the first questionnaire. The r between personalism and protest was .01. The high-protest quartile had a mean personalism score of 3.65; the low-protest quartile had a mean personalism score of 3.66. However, we shall not dismiss the hypothesis but will return to it in the analysis of change in Chapters VII and VIII.

SOCIAL TYPES AND PROTEST

In Schrag's analysis of social types, he used a sociometric method of classifying inmates into the type categories.[7] Inmate judges were asked to nominate inmates for the categories. Schrag's report on the characteristics of the types was based on interviewing of those inmates on whom the judges agreed. The present analysis of types is based on the self-conceptions of the inmates, and not on ratings by others.

In the scoring method shown in Appendix B, the reader will note that for each of the types a different one of the seven self-conception items was given double weight. These will serve as convenient reminders of the type characteristics and are as follows:

Square John: "The only criminals I really know are the ones here inside the

Reformatory."

<u>Con politician</u>: "I am clever in getting what I want from Reformatory officials."
<u>Outlaw</u>: "It makes me sore to have people tell me what to do."
<u>Right guy</u>: "If other inmates are counting on me, I'll do my best for the inmates in this place."

The social types have an important place in the analysis that follows. There are a number of reasons for this choice. Schrag's original study, followed by the works of Kinch,[8] Garabedian,[9] and Garrity,[10] give us an excellent analysis of some of the characteristics of these types. Second, these analyses have shown that the four types above represent stable roles centered around important focal issues in prison life. Thus, we can expect to relate them to a good many other variables. In a sense, the social types play the same part in analysis of a prison that social class plays in other areas of sociology. Social types serve as an important and stable attribute to which a great many qualities may be inferred. Further, the discovery of relations between the social types and protest gives one the assurance of having made a discovery which will be fruitful in the future.

First let us look at some validating data on our social type measure. Schrag[11] found a relationship between his types, measured sociometrically, and criminal career characteristics. Square Johns were found to have little previous institutional experience, right guys had long previous records, con politicians had some previous institutional experience but less than right guys. Outlaws were similar to con politicians; some were first offenders and some were recidivists. Furthermore, right guys more than others had a tendency to have previous juvenile commitments. Table XVI shows data on criminal career.

Our findings about the square John type are consistent with Schrag's findings. The findings on the right guy and on the con politician show them to be similar, given an allowance for sampling variability. The right guy shows a lesser tendency to be arrested before the age of 14, but also a lesser tendency to have a first arrest at the age of 18 or thereafter. Both right guys and con politicians tend to have early arrests and institutionalization, but the outlaw has the strongest tendency in this direction. This finding about outlaws is somewhat inconsistent with Schrag's findings, although Garabedian's findings were similar to those reported here.[12]

Thus our social type measure bears some relation, not perfect, to previous studies. What is the relation of social type characteristics to protest? We hypothesized the following:

1. <u>Square Johns</u> are expected to have the lowest protest scores. Since they accept legitimate values, they will not see the demands made by staff members as personal in character but as requests that they themselves would make if they were staff members. They also are likely to value the exchanges that staff can give--school, vocational training, etc.--and are likely to perceive the staff as sympathetic.

Table XVI

Relationship of Social Types to Previous Criminal Experiences

Social type	Percent of social type having one or more juvenile commitments	Percent of social type having at least one arrest before age 14	Percent of social type first arrested at age 18 or later	N
Square john	41	27	35	37
Con politician	62	40	32	40
Outlaw	70	60	30	10
Right guy	57	33	17	30

Data taken from second questionnaire.

2. <u>Con politicians</u> are expected to have protest scores somewhat higher than those of square Johns. Although they do not identify with legitimate values, they are oriented toward manipulation and will be constrained to avoid building up a negative relation with the staff.

3. <u>Outlaws</u> are expected to have the highest protest scores. The outlaw type is basically defined in terms of unwillingness to comply with the demands of authority.

4. <u>Right guys</u> will have protest scores lower than outlaws but higher than politicians. They perceive the demands of staff members as illegitimate--they may have a greater tendency to do this than outlaws, since right guys are probably receiving more consistent support for an anti-social ideology. Thus every demand of the staff is perceived as the desire to subordinate the inmate to staff wishes. However, the right guys also are said to put some emphasis on calm, deliberate behavior and so are less likely to engage in the extremes of conflict behavior that characterize the outlaws.

Table XVII gives the data on social types and protest. The data are taken from Questionnaire Three. The type instrument was first used on Questionnaire Two, but a shortened version of the protest scale was used on that questionnaire. The longer version of the scale is probably more reliable.

The results shown in Table XVII conform to the predictions. However, two points should be noted. First a big difference occurs between the square Johns and the other types. Con politicians are much closer to right guys than to square Johns. Second, the mean for outlaws is based on only seven cases (our scoring system produced relatively few outlaws). On Questionnaire Two, the right guys had a slightly higher protest score than did the outlaws. The safest conclusion is that right guys and outlaws are both high on protest.

Table XVII

Protest Scores of Four Social Types

Social type	Mean protest score	N
Square John	20.7	23
Con politician	26.9	43
Outlaw	32.0	7
Right guy	28.0	36

Probability that the group of means above is drawn from a common population $<.01$. (F test, $F = 8.96$)

Data taken from third questionnaire.

SOCIAL TYPES AND PERSONALISM

For purposes of later analysis, we shall ask whether or not there are differences between the types with respect to personalism scores. Table XVIII gives the percentages for the four types.

Table XVIII

Social Types and Personalism

Social type	Percent having high personalism score	N
Square John	40	35
Con politician	54	39
Outlaw	20	10
Right guy	31	26

High personalism = score of 5-8. For this table, the personalism score used was computed by summing the scores on all questionnaires and converting to a 1-8 point scale

Data taken from second questionnaire.

SOCIAL TYPES AND INSTRUMENTALISM

As mentioned in Chapter IV, analysis of the instrumentalism scale did not yield promising results. The instrumentalism scale was designed to measure the tendency of inmates to change their protesting or accommodating responses in the face of rewards for changed responses; the scale is supposed to measure the tendency to <u>negotiate for reward</u>. The distribution of scale scores suggested that many inmates were responding to the items in idiosyncratic terms. Instead of relying on an overall score, it was decided to rank the types on each item, asking which type received the highest instrumentalism rank, next highest, etc. on each item. This approach served to partially eliminate the large score variance due to idiosyncratic responses. Table XIX shows the results of this analysis.

Outlaws have the highest overall instrumentalism rank on the items, con politicians second, square Johns third, and right guys the lowest instrumentalism rank. The finding that right guys are lowest is not surprising. Cressey and Irwin anticipate this finding in their discussion of the difference between the separate subcultures of the "thief" and the "convict."[13] They suggested that the "convict" is oriented toward maximizing his privileges, usually illicit, in the institution. The "thief" is oriented toward "doing his time" with a minimum of involvement in the rackets of the prison. He is oriented toward the outside, criminal culture. Cressey and Irwin suggest that the right guy is closest to the thief type and the con politician closest to the convict type. Cressey and Irwin do not anticipate the finding that outlaws are the most willing to negotiate for privilege. Apparently our earlier suggestion that outlaws cope with their situation of low dominance by withdrawing from negotiation with the staff was incorrect. The attitude of withdrawal seems to characterize the right guys, not the outlaws. Furthermore, the data on instrumentalism suggests that the square John is like the right guy; he is not instrumental, but rather is moral in outlook.

These data suggest that the outlaws are oriented toward establishing their dominance in prison activities to a greater degree than are con politicians. A comparison of the responses of con politicians and outlaws to item 3 is instructive. Outlaws got a much higher score on this item than did con politicians, whose score was close to that of the right guys. The item read:

At a reformatory they were having official visitors from the state capitol. The food had not been too good lately, but on this day they were getting fried chicken. The staff quietly passed the word around that they wanted everyone to look good for the visitors. If they didn't, the warden probably would get irritated and cut privileges. A bunch of inmates started to push and shove in the line while the visitors were watching.

How do you personally feel about the inmates' actions?

The item presents an unsympathetic, unconcerned warden who uses punishment to get his way. His reason for giving the inmates fried chicken is to please the visitors, not the inmates. The outlaw accepts this behavior as a determinant of his strategy. The con politician rejects it. We hypothesize that the difference between

Table XIX

Responses of Four Social Types to the Instrumentalism Scale

Social type	Item 1 Mean	Item 1 Rank	Item 2 Mean	Item 2 Rank	Item 3 Mean	Item 3 Rank	Item 4 Mean	Item 4 Rank	Overall mean rank	Overall rank	Total scale score	N
Square John	1.51	2	1.57	4	2.8	1	3.11	3	2.6	3	8.11	37
Con politician	1.42	3	2.20	1	2.05	3	3.22	1	2.0	2	8.92	40
Outlaw	1.7	1	1.80	3	2.5	2	3.20	2	1.8	1	9.20	10
Right guy	1.28	4	2.07	2	2.03	4	2.86	4	3.6	4	8.24	29

1 = highest possible rank; 4 = highest possible instrumentalism score

Data taken from first questionnaire.

the types rests on the assumptions that the politician type must make for effective role performance. His style of relationship to the staff requires that they be manipulatable by interpersonal tactics--by the tactic of winning the staff's good opinion, for example. The outlaw has a highly negative perception of the attitudes of the staff toward inmates. His style of negotiation does not require attraction between the parties as a condition for success. In short, the outlaws' basis for negotiation is reward; the con politician's basis for negotiation is sympathy.

Two pieces of data reinforce our picture of the con politician. First, the data on the personalism scale gave the con politician a high personalism score. Con politicians tend to believe that others do things for reasons of friendship or hostility. Thus it is only the manipulation of friendship that will gain compliance. On the other hand, outlaws have quite low personalism scores. Second, con politicians have considerably higher scores on sympathy than do the outlaws. The means are 16.2 and 14.0, respectively. Con politicians see staff members as more sympathetic than do outlaws. However, we are not suggesting that outlaws see the staff as rewarding; it is just that if the staff offered rewards, they might comply.

This suggests the striking possibility that, in the face of a very hostile staff, the con politicians and outlaws would tend to switch roles, with the former expressing greatest hostility toward the staff. The data above, at any rate, press us toward the conclusion that both are quite strongly oriented toward the prison's major symbol of dominance, the maintenance of privilege.

SUMMARY

In this chapter we have looked at the social-psychological world of inmates. Consistent patterns have appeared in this world. Protesting inmates tend to have a harsh picture of staff attitudes. Few exceptions exist to their image that staff members are negative and unyielding in their view of inmates. Accommodating inmates, on the other hand, believe that staff members have a positive, yielding, compliant view of inmates and are willing to reward the inmates' efforts to conform. Inmates who picture themselves as outlaws or right guys are quite protesting in their responses. Only the square Johns have a clear tendency to accommodate, although certain possibilities for accommodation appear in the responses of con politicians and outlaws to the instrumentalism scale. The picture of oneself as a con politician seems to require the picture of the staff as sympathetic and tolerant of inmates, although it does not require the picture of oneself as sympathetic to the staff. Protest appears to increase certain aspects of identification with inmates, although it neither increases "liking" nor produces positive perceptions of many attributes of inmates. Like the victims of the natural disasters discussed in Chapter III, the "victims," of the staff come to feel a great sense of unity, but not necessarily a great sense of power.

FOOTNOTES

[1] Charles E. Osgood, George J. Suci, and Percy H. Tennenbaum, *The Measurement of Meaning* (Urbana, Ill.: The University of Illinois Press, 1957).

[2] The semantic differential word pairs were developed from the original Osgood material by Dr. Herbert Costner of the University of Washington.

[3] Richard McCleery, "The Governmental Process and Informal Social Control" in Donald Cressey (ed.), *The Prison* (New York: Holt, Rinehart, and Winston, Inc., 1961), p. 154.

[4] Ibid.

[5] Alvin Gouldner, *Patterns of Industrial Bureaucracy* (Glencoe, Ill.: The Free Press, 1954), pp. 164-166. According to Gouldner, the opposite of the "screening function" in the "leeway function"; in the latter case, the supervisor uses his ability to relax the rules as a control technique.

[6] A.M. Henderson and Talcott Parson (eds.), Max Weber, *The Theory of Social and Economic Organization* (New York: Oxford University Press, 1947), p. 337.

[7] Clarence C. Schrag, "Social Types in a Prison Community" (unpublished Master's thesis, University of Washington, Seattle, 1944), pp. 56-57.

[8] John W. Kinch, "Certain Social Psychological Aspects of Types of Juvenile Delinquents" (unpublished Ph.D. dissertation, University of Washington, Seattle, 1959).

[9] Peter G. Garabedian, "Western Penitentiary: A Study in Social Organization" (unpublished Ph.D. dissertaion, University of Washington, Seattle, 1959).

[10] Donald Garrity, "The Prison as a Rehabilitation Agency" in Donald Cressey (ed.), *The Prison* (New York: Holt, Rinehart, and Winston, Inc., 1961).

[11] Schrag, op. cit., Chapters 5, 6, 7, and 8.

[12] Garabedian, op. cit., p. 109.

[13] Donald R. Cressey and John Irwin, "Thieves, Convicts, and the Inmate Culture," *Social Problems*, X:2 (Fall, 1962), 142-145.

CHAPTER VII

THE STRUCTURAL CORRELATES OF PROTEST

SOCIAL STRUCTURE AND CONFLICT

Analysis of perceptual data does not provide a complete understanding of conflict behavior. From such data we may learn something about certain social-psychological processes in the abstract. To root these processes to concrete social experience, it is desirable to look at the effect of prison organization on inmates. How do formal social position and informal social relations affect behavior? We shall try to interpret these organizational factors as social-psychological stimuli. For example, does a given position expose its occupants to a set of perceptions that determine their relationship to the staff? Finally a look at the effect of time in prison on perception and behavior may tell us whether there is a cumulative effect of prison experiences among inmates.

PREVIOUS CRIMINAL EXPERIENCES AND PROTEST

Earlier we found that there was some relation between one aspect of an inmate's self-conception--his social type--and previous experience with arrest and commitment. Social type was related to protest scores. Perhaps things are pretty much decided by the time an inmate arrives in an adult institution and few of the events that occur inside have much effect on protest. Table XX shows the effect of some criminal career factors on protest.

Inspection of Table XX does not show any substantial relationship between protest and age at first arrest, juvenile commitments, or number of arrests. Although Table XX indicates a slight downward trend in amount of experience in moving from the high-protest quartile to medium low, the low-protest quartile reverses the trend. The low and high-protest quartiles have about equal amounts of criminal experience, juding from this table. Plainly, Table XX offers promise that experience in this particular reformatory may be the important determinant of inmate behavior toward the reformatory staff.

The relationship between social type and criminal career characteristics may make the absence of a relationship in Table XX seem a bit perplexing. The negative

Table XX

Relationship of Previous Criminal Experiences and Protest

Protest quartiles	Criminal Experiences Percent of quartile having one or more juvenile commitments		Percent of quartile having three or more previous arrests		Percent of quartile having at least one arrest before age 14	
	Percent	N	Percent	N	Percent	N
High	57	(35)	65	(37)	43	(37)
Medium high	51	(37)	61	(38)	35	(37)
Medium low	46	(41)	55	(42)	30	(40)
Low	57	(35)	63	(35)	43	(35)

N = number of inmates in quartile, excluding those who did not respond to the question.

Data taken from third questionnaire.

finding is easily understood, however, when it is remembered that there was considerable variation in the criminal career characteristics within the type categories. For example, 41 percent of the square Johns had at least one juvenile commitment. Within the limits imposed by the pattern of experience with law-enforcement agencies, there apparently is ample opportunity for an adjustment that is unique to the particular institution.

STATUS AND PROTEST

Inmates responded to an instrument which asked them to rate the "desirability" or "undesirability" of the different institutional work crews. The details of the scoring are given in Appendix B. Mean ratings were computed for each work crew. We then ranked all the work crews and divided them so that approximately one-third of the inmates in the total prison population fell into each of three categories. The categories are high, medium, and low status. "High," of course, refers to the jobs perceived to be most desirable.

For this particular instrument we had the opportunity to compare the responses of our sample, relatively representative with respect to time served, to a sample of 65 inmates who were within the first two months of the beginning of their sentences. The latter 65 inmates were either still in the reception and guidance unit or just released to the main population. The correlation between the ranks was .01.[1] This high relationship between the two groups probably indicates that there is a rather stable order to these ratings. This finding was unexpected, since the main population inmates and the newly-arrived inmates presumably differ considerably in their knowledge of prison jobs and the inmate status system. The correlation of ranks is probably a function of the fact that there are some "universal" values related to these jobs, perhaps prestige in the outside community. Academic school and vocational training rate high, yard work and menial labor rate low, reflecting the same evaluations such activities may receive from ordinary citizens.

Job status is one of the important rewards that the prison staff can give an inmate. Some jobs offer pleasant working conditions, others offer hourly pay, some offer illicit payment (it is said that barbers may receive "tips" for special services), some jobs offer training for outside specialties. Do these rewards induce compliant behavior?

One kind of answer to the above question is given by examination of the effect of money payment. The furniture factory and the mattress factory are both industries and at the time of the study were among the very few jobs that provided money payment. They both received a low rank by our inmates. The furniture factory was seventh from the bottom and the mattress factory fourth from the bottom. It might seem surprising that inmates ranked paying jobs very low, since many of them are badly in need of money. A tentative explanation of this phenomenon is based on the chain of relationships that occur when an inmate decides to earn money by working in a prison industry.

Wages in the mattress and furniture factories begin at two cents per hour and increase to 14 cents per hour. Many inmates consider it degrading to work for such a small amount of money. Moreover, if they are to get a rate much above two cents an hour, it is necessary to please the supervisor by demonstrating hard work. In short, to earn money they must get involved in interaction which they may regard as degrading. The rewards are small, but the conformity required is high. On the other hand, a barber is a student; barbering is a vocational school. The student is not doing his work for money payment but because his own wish is to become a barber. In addition, he may receive money from other inmates. Inmates do care about money, but they appear to withdraw from the money offers of the staff because of the status degradation which accepting money may entail.

Money thus seems to have failed as a reward. However, since there are wide differences in job status, the staff can also give status rewards to inmates. We have, in effect, a measure of the real social value of these rewards, rather than any value attributed by wages. According to our theory, individuals who receive rewards should be more willing to conform, because the reward produces a more favorable exchange relationship for them. Of course, the exception to this is produced when the reward carries with it a demand for increased conformity. Table XXI summarizes the data on job status and protest.

The results of this table are surprising. No consistent relationship between job status and protest, negative or positive, is seen. If one had not started with any

Table XXI

Relationship Between Work Crew Status and Protest Scores

Work Crew Status Level	Mean Protest Score	N
High	25.8	80
Medium	27.3	57
Low	25.8	23

The probability that means are drawn from a common population $>.05$.
(F test, F = .63)

Data taken from first questionnaire.

theoretical hypothesis, one would still expect the prison staff to select an inmate for a job on the basis of the inmate's attitude; the staff is well aware of the major outlines of the status hierarchy. The negative finding suggests that staff decisions are made on the basis of some professional standard--not, "Does the inmate deserve it?" but rather, "Does he need it?" We shall return to job status in our analysis of change data.

INFORMAL SOCIAL RELATIONS AND PROTEST

As described earlier, the "friendship" instrument asked the inmate to respond to a series of questions about the characteristics of specific friends. The responses were scored to produce the social type category prevailing among the friends.

Our theory outlined a number of mechanisms by which the behavior of others may be controlled. To summarize:

1. Norms may be defined in informal groups so as to increase the likelihood that an inmate will see staff demands as different from his own desires. Thus, the unfavorableness of the exchange may increase for the inmate, thereby increasing his tendency to engage in conflict behavior.

2. The informal group may provide the inmate with a negative picture of the staff's attitude toward inmates, thereby decreasing the favorableness of the exchange with the staff.

3. The informal group may pay a great deal of attention to the symbolic meaning of interaction for the position of dominance-subordination held by any given inmate. This mechanism of control is hypothesized to reduce the inmate's tendency to engage in public acts of accommodation; it will be called the "audience effect."

These hypothesized mechanisms lead us to predict that protesting inmates will present stimuli to their inmate friends which will serve to increase the friends' protesting tendency. In effect, the protesting inmate controls the behavior of others by projecting his own view of the staff into the social milieu.

FRIENDS' SOCIAL TYPE AND PROTEST

No data are available on actual or perceived protest scores of the inmate's friends, but inferences can be made from the social type characteristics. Since the square John, for example, has markedly lower protest scores than other types, it is hypothesized that inmates whose friends are predominantly square Johns will have lower protest scores than will those whose friends are of the other three types. Table XXII shows the relation between friends' type characteristics and protest scores.

Table XXII shows a negative relationship between having square John friends and protest, as hypothesized. The relationship, however, is a weak one. A much stronger relationship exists between having outlaw friends and high protest scores. While the data are generally in support of our hypothesis, they do not clearly confirm the operation of the mechanisms described above.

Table XXII

Relationship Between Perceived Characteristics
of Friends and Protest Scores

Inmates' protest quartile	Square John (N = 21) Percent	Con politician (N = 27) Percent	Outlaw (N = 16) Percent	Right guy (N = 25) Percent
High	10	30	44	32
Medium high	33	22	44	16
Medium low	19	30	6	24
Low	38	19	6	28
	100*	100	100	100

Prevailing type among friends

*Due to rounding errors, not all percentages add to exactly 100.

Data taken from second questionnaire.

A TEST OF THE AUDIENCE EFFECT

A separate test of the third mechanism, the audience effect, is possible. On the basis of our findings in Chapter VI, it is possible to classify the social types as dominance or non-dominance oriented. Our analysis of the instrumentalism scale found that con politicians and outlaws ranked highest in the tendency to be oriented toward gaining privilege by manipulating the staff--to be oriented toward negotiated reward. Earlier it was argued that concern with negotiated reward produces movement into the dominance dimension. If we assume that this hypothesis is a correct one, we can classify the social types as to their dominance orientation. The outlaws and con politicians were classified as dominance oriented because of their concern with negotiated reward, and the non-instrumental right guys and square Johns were classified as non-dominance oriented.

A matrix of four categories can be established by cross-classifying orientation of self against orientation of friends. The four categories are:

1. *Dominance-oriented self, dominance-oriented friends*: Includes outlaws or con politicians who have outlaw or con politician friends.

2. *Non-dominance-oriented self, dominance-oriented friends*: Includes right guys or square Johns who have outlaw or con politician friends.

3. *Dominance-oriented self, non-dominance-oriented friends*: Includes outlaws or con politicians who have right guy or square John friends.

4. *Non-dominance-oriented self, non-dominance-oriented friends*: Includes right guys or square Johns who have right guy or square John friends.

It is predicted that Type 1 will have the highest protest score since both personal orientations and those of friends predispose toward scrutinizing interactions with staff in terms of the symbolic meaning of the interaction for dominance. Conversely, the lack of such scrutiny should produce the lowest protest score for Type 4. Types 2 and 3 will fall in between the other two, but it is not clear from our theory whether Type 2 or Type 3 will have the higher score. Table XXIII summarizes the data on the self-friends matrix and protest scores.

The data from Table XXIII are striking.[2] As predicted, Type 4 has the lowest protest score, and Type 1 has the highest score.

The findings on the intermediate types are especially intriguing. There is only a small difference in scores between Type 3 and Type 4, but a large difference between Type 2 and Type 4. In these data the orientation of friends has a far greater effect on protest score than one's own orientation. The lowest score occurs for those inmates who are themselves lacking in dominance orientation and whose friends have a similar orientation. If we vary the orientation of self only, we find that protest goes up little in the case of the inmate who is dominance oriented but whose friends are not dominance oriented. If we vary the orientation of friends only, we find that protest

Table XXIII

Relationship Between Self-Friends Matrix and Protest Score

Type	Self orientation	Friends orientation	Mean protest score	N*
1.........	Dominance	Dominance	28.9	14
2.........	Non-dominance	Dominance	26.0	17
3.........	Dominance	Non-dominance	23.5	13
4.........	Non-dominance	Non-dominance	23.0	22

*The small N's are due to a number of individuals who had tied scores between two or more self or friends type categories and had to be eliminated from use in the analysis.

Probability that means were drawn from a common population $>.05$. (F test, F = 1.79)

Data on protest and self orientation taken from third questionnaire.
Data on friends orientation taken from second questionnaire.

goes up considerably for those whose friends are dominance oriented but who are not dominance oriented themselves. However, it should not be assumed that the orientation of self is unimportant. A comparison of Type 2 and Type 1 shows that protest goes up considerably as self changes from non-dominance to dominance orientation, if friends are dominance oriented.

We conclude that the foregoing provides some confirmation of the "audience effect" and of the hypothesis stating that concern with negotiated reward leads to a dominance orientation. The view an inmate's friend takes of his behavior appears to exercise more control over his public behavior--measured by the protest score--than does the view he himself takes of the behavior. Type 2 has the second highest protest score, even though about half the inmates in that type are square Johns. In contrast, none of the inmates in Type 3 are square Johns.

A different interpretation can be placed on these data by arguing that the inmate's friends control his behavior by changing his private view of the staff and not just his public behavior. Table XXIV summarizes the data on self-friends matrix and sympathy--the perception inmates have of the sympathy that staff members display toward inmates.

No consistent relationship is found in Table XXIV. The variations in the public protest behavior, found in Table XXIII, are not reflected in the private view of the staff by the four categories of inmates. The technique of control demonstrated in this table appears to be effective in the control of public behavior but not in the control of private views of the staff. To summarize, we find consistent support for the hypothesis that a major factor in accounting for variations in protest is the perceptions inmates

Table XXIV

Relationship Between Self-Friends Matrix and Sympathy Score

Type	Self orientation	Friends orientation	Mean sympathy score	N
1.........	Dominance	Dominance	16.7	14
2.........	Non-dominance	Dominance	14.7	17
3.........	Dominance	Non-dominance	17.8	13
4.........	Non-dominance	Non-dominance	16.5	22

Probability that means are drawn from a common population $>.05$. (F test, F = .87)
Data taken from third questionnaire.

have as to how their friends will respond to their behavior. Accommodating behavior may degrade the inmate's public status, even though his private view of the staff does not make accommodation an unfavorable exchange for him.

TIME SERVED AND PROTEST

Is there a cumulative effect of participation in the typical informal social relations among inmates or between inmates and staff? Table XXV summarizes the effect of length of time served on protest and sympathy scores.

Protest shows a weak and variable trend in an upward direction; sympathy shows a variable trend in a downward direction. Using statistical independence as an index of the strength of the relationship, the relation between sympathy and time served would seem to be the stronger of the two.

We are using time served as an index of the effect of time on inmates. Unfortunately, it is also an index to the seriousness of the offense or the decisions of the parole board concerning the inmates' chances of success on parole. Thus, any conclusions from time served are bound to be shaky. For example, an inmate may have served a long time in consequence of a highly negative attitude toward the staff. Perhaps for the foregoing reasons, previous studies have indicated that inmate attitudes vary more clearly with position in the institutional cycle of admission to discharge than such attitudes do with regard to chronological time served.[3]

Table XXVI shows the relationship between sympathy, protest, and time in the institutional career phase of admission to discharge.

Table XXVI shows a linear relationship between position in institutional career

-93-

Table XXV

Relationships Between Time served and Protest
and Sympathy Scores

Time served	Mean protest score	Mean sympathy score	N
2 - 4 months*	24.6	19.1	14
4 - 8 months*	25.9	16.4	53
8 - 12 months*	26.7	15.1	19
12 - 16 months*	25.5	17.0	44
16 - 24 months*	26.3	14.2	21
24 months or more*	29.3	14.4	19

*The upper limit of each time category should read "under x months." Thus, an inmate who had served three months and 29 days would be put in the first category; an inmate who had served exactly four months would do in the second category.

For the protest scores, the probability that the means are drawn from a common population $>$ .05. (F test, F = .76) For the sympathy scores the probability that the means are drawn from a common population $>$ .05. (F test, F = 1.71)

Data taken from first questionnaire.

phase until four months before discharge when protest decreases and sympathy increases. It is difficult to know whether this reversal at the end of the cycle represents a significant trend, as it is based on only nine cases. It is not anticipated by any change in the marked, upward trend for the preceding periods and may not indicate a genuine reversal in the linear trend.

On the other hand, the studies just cited provide strong evidence of decreases in the unfavorability of attitudes that we cautiously noted near the end of the institutional career.[4] These studies uniformly found that inmate attitudes toward the staff became increasingly negative until the last stages of the institutional career, when they became more positive.

For most of the time periods during their institutional careers, the inmates in our study acquired an increasingly negative view of the staff, which tended to be reflected in increasingly protesting behavior.

Table XXVI

Relationships Between Institutional Career Phase and
Sympathy and Protest Scores

Phase	Mean protest score	Mean sympathy score	N
Early:			
4 - 8 months served	25.8	17.6	18
Middle:	26.1	15.8	70
Late:*			
6-8 months to release	27.3	15.0	15
4-6 months to release	31.4	13.2	12
0-4 months to release	24.2	19.0	9

* "6-8 months to release" means 6 months to <u>less than</u> 8 months; the other categories follow the same procedure.

For the protest scores, the probability that the means are drawn from a common population $>$ .05. (F test, F = 1.73) For the sympathy scores, the probability that the means are drawn from a common population $>$ .05. (F test, F = 2.24; p = .05 when F = 2.42)

Data taken from third questionnaire.

PERSONALISM, TIME SERVED, AND PROTEST

In Chapter VI no confirmation was obtained for the hypothesis that <u>personalism</u> is positively related to <u>protest</u>. Exploratory study of the data indicated that the effect of personalism might interact with the effect of time. Subsequent analysis of the data substantiated what was, at first, no more than a guess. Table XXVII shows the effect of time on inmates low and high on personalism. Table XXVIII shows the same relationships for the sympathy variable.

Inmates who are initially high on personalism show a substantial increase in protest as chronological time served increases. No such relationship is observed for those low on personalism. This finding comes close to being significant at the .05 level; we shall tentatively assume it to be a stable finding. Again, inmates high on personalism show a significant downward relationship between sympathy and time served, while those low on personalism show no consistent trend.

Tables XXVII and XXVIII suggest that an inmate's institutional career will be quite different if he is high on personalism from that of an inmate who is low on

-95-

Table XXVII

Relationship Between Time Served and Protest Scores,
Controlled for Level of Personalism

Time served	Mean protest score	N
High personalism level:		
2 - 4 months	23.4	7
4 - 8 months	23.0	28
8 - 16 months	25.9	26
16 - 24 months	26.7	12
24 months or more	30.4	14
Low personalism level:		
2 - 4 months	25.7	7
4 - 8 months	29.2	25
8 - 16 months	25.6	36
16 - 24 months	25.7	9
24 months or more	26.2	5

For those <u>high</u> on personalism, the probability that means are drawn from a common population $>.05$. (F test, F = 2.42; p = .05 when F = 2.48)

For those <u>low</u> on personalism, the probability that means are drawn from a common population $>.05$. (F test, F = .81)

Data taken from first questionnaire.

personalism. The typical events that occur in the institution tend to produce an increasingly negative view of the staff. However, this process apparently occurs among only the personalistic and not the impersonalistic inmates. Personalistic inmates seem to interpret events in a way that makes the staff appear increasingly hostile.

Much interaction between staff and inmate centers around the carrying out of orders. Earlier, it was shown that even accommodating inmates tend to resent the institutional rules. Apparently, the only way in which the personalistic inmate can explain these repeated unpleasant demands upon himself is by assuming that the staff is unsympathetic toward him. We conclude that this process involves the inmate in a pattern of protest behavior toward the staff.

One anomalous finding is that personalistic inmates are initially <u>lower</u> on protest and higher on sympathy than are impersonalistic inmates. This finding was not anticipated in the theory. The various findings on personalism are quite important to the theory and will be examined in greater detail in Chapter VIII.

Table XXVIII

Relationship Between Time Served and Sympathy Scores,
Controlled for Level of Personalism

Time Served	Mean sympathy score	N
High personalism level:		
2 - 4 months	22.9	7
4 - 8 months	17.5	28
8 - 16 months	16.3	26
16 - 24 months	15.7	12
24 months or more	13.9	14
Low personalism level:		
2 - 4 months	15.4	7
4 - 8 months	15.0	25
8 - 16 months	16.6	36
16 - 24 months	12.2	9
24 months or more	16.0	5

For those <u>high</u> on personalism, the probability that the means are drawn from a common population $<$ .05. (F test, F = 2.77)

For those <u>low</u> on personalism, the probability that the means are drawn from a common population $>$ .05. (F test, F = 1.06)

Data taken from first questionnaire.

SUMMARY

In this chapter we examined a number of relationships between structural factors and protest. No evidence was found of any static correlation between protest and penal experience or work crew status. A relatively weak correlation was found between protest and the prevailing perceived social type among the inmates' friends. When the friends' social types were categorized in terms of dominance orientation, a stronger and more predictable relation was found. Evidence supporting the hypothesis that concern with negotiated reward leads to dominance orientation and the hypothesis that dominance orientation leads to conflict was provided by the "self-friends matrix." Data on time suggest that protest increases with the length of the individual's stay in the institution, but that this effect depends on how the inmate interprets typical life events.

Finally, the lack of correlation between job status and protest, the weak correlation between friends' social type and protest, and the relatively strong correlation between time and protest, under some circumstances, suggest that static correlations may not be the best tool for looking at the effects of social structure. The effects of structure may be cumulative and not apparent in the short run. Analysis of change data will show whether this hunch is a correct one.

FOOTNOTES

[1] Spearman's rho.

[2] However, they are not statistically significant. The question of how stable they are should be put off until the data on change are examined for a parallel.

[3] Stanton Wheeler, "Socialization in Correctional Communities," American Sociological Review, XXVI (October, 1961), 699-712; Daniel Glaser and John R. Stratton, "Measuring Change in Prison" in Donald R. Cressey (ed.), The Prison (New York: Holt, Rinehart, and Winston, Inc., 1961), Chapter 10; Peter O. Garabedian, "Social Roles and the Process of Socialization in a Prison Community," Social Problems, XI (Fall, 1963), 139-152.

[4] Wheeler, op. cit.; Glaser and Stratton, op. cit.; Garabedian, op. cit.

CHAPTER VIII

METHODOLOGICAL PROBLEMS IN THE ANALYSIS OF CHANGE

Three months intervened between the administration of the first and third questionnaires. It was hoped that during this period scores on a number ov variables would show variation that reflected changes in the level of the variable rather than random changes due to scale unreliability.

Change scores were computed by subtracting the initial score from the terminal score and adding a constant number so as to bring all scores above zero. On the protest change measure, for example, a score of 25 indicates identical scores at the initial and terminal times. A score above 25 indicates that the inmate's score has increased; a score below 25 indicates a decrease. In the case of instruments where the number of items was changed between the two administrations, "no change" means that no change occurred other than that due to the difference in the number of items. In discussing change computations, "Time One" refers to data gathered from Questionnaire One (on June 26, approximately), "Time Two" refers to Questionnaire Two (given on August 1, approximately), and "Time Three" refers to Questionnaire Three (given on September 20, approximately).

The correlation between protest at Time One and protest change at Time Two was -.88.[1] In other words, approximately 77.5 percent of the variation in change scores could be accounted for by the initial level of protest, if one predicted that the higher the initial score, the lower the change score (i.e., the more downward change would occur), and vice versa, the lower the initial score, the higher the change score.

We could think of no sociological reason for the above correlation. The technical problems seemed to account for the correlation. The first problem was related to differences in the scale variances; the second problem arose from what can be called a "regression toward the mean" phenomenon.

THE PROBLEM OF DIFFERENTIAL SCALE VARIANCE

The protest scale contained 15 items at Time One but only 6 items at Time Two. This difference resulted in a variance of 62.1 for the larger version, but only 13.7 for the shorter version of the scale; (the standard deviations were 7.88 and 3.20

respectively). In consequence, when the scores on the scale with the large variance are subtracted from the scores on the scale with the small variance, the differences are largely a function of the scale with the greater variance. This can easily be understood by imagining the variance to be zero at Time Two, i.e., everybody having the same score. In that case the change scores would be the same as the original scores, minus the constant score received at Time Two. Since we subtracted the first score from the second, the sign of the difference would be reversed and the correlation between the initial score and the change score would be -1.00.

Thus, it is necessary that some adjustment be made in order to give both scores, those at Time One and at Time Two, an equal opportunity to influence the change score.

THE PROBLEM OF REGRESSION TOWARD THE MEAN

If the variances of both the initial and the terminal measures are identical, it is still likely that there will be negative correlation between initial level and change scores. The correlation results from the tendency of individuals below the mean to move up and those above the mean to move down. As McNemar points out, this phenomenon may be a function of no more than scale unreliability.[2] He points out that if the scales had a form-to-form reliability coefficient of .85, the correlation between initial level and change would be -.27. A common-sense explanation of this phenomenon can be easily grasped by considering the extreme lows and high in the scale. In the case of normally distributed scores, the probability of anyone receiving a higher or lower score diminishes rapidly at the extremes. Random variation due to errors of measurement is likely to cause the scores of the extreme cases to change in the direction of the mean.

The reliability coefficient for protest, at Time One, was .66.[3] Thus we can expect considerable correlation between initial level and change, as a result of unreliability.

McNemar suggests that the reliability coefficients of the two measures be used to compute a theoretical regression line between initial level and change.[4] This regression line can then be used to arrive at "regressed" scores by subtracting the predicted score from the actual score. The regressed scores represent variation not due to initial levels. However, McNemar's technique requires the calculation of an interscale reliability coefficient, a task for which we did not have adequate data.[5]

Instead of attempting to use McNemar's technique, it was decided to compute the actual regression line between initial level and change, and to use this line to compute regressed scores. Like McNemar's technique, our technique compensates for the differences between the scale variances as well as regression toward the mean. Our technique, however, requires the assumption that there is no real movement toward the mean, i.e., that all of the correlation between initial level and change in an artifact of unreliability. While there is no feasible way of testing this assumption, it can be made with reasonable safety for these data. If the assumption is incorrect, it results only in our not being able to analyze the valid change toward the mean that did occur.

COMPUTATION OF REGRESSED SCORES

Regressed scores were computed for our two major variables, namely, protest change and sympathy-reward change (the sum of sympathy and reward). We shall report only the change between Time One and Time Three, as it appeared that there was not sufficient variation by Time Two to justify analysis. The unadjusted correlation between protest level at Time One and change by Time Three was -.48,[6] and the variances were 62.3 and 53.29, respectively.[7]

The meaning of the regressed change scores should be kept clearly in mind. If an individual started with an extremely low protest score and did not move upward, he would have been recorded as having some degree of downward change, since it was predicted that his score would change upward. The reverse is also true; a high-scoring inmate who did not move downward would be recorded as having some degree of upward change. The predicted score was subtracted from the actual score, rounded to the nearest digit, and increased by a constant sufficient to make all numbers larger than zero. Appendix C shows the predicted values, rounded. For sympathy change, a score of 4 indicates no change. For protest change, a score of 25 indicates no change.[8]

It is of interest to note what happens when the regressed scores, or some substitute, are not used. Ashley Weeks, in his study of the Highfields Project,[9] measured changes in a number of attitudes that were supposed to be related to post-institutional adjustment, but he did not use regressed scores. In his analysis, Weeks found that the boys at Highfields, by and large, changed in an unfavorable direction, as compared to a comparison group at the more custody-oriented Annandale institution nearby, even though the Highfields boys achieved greater success on parole.[10] Since the boys at Highfields were selected on the basis of suitability for treatment and were initially more favorable on the above-mentioned attitude variables, it is likely that regression toward the mean was confounding the results. That is, the boys at Highfields, initially high on the variables, had a tendency to change downward toward the mean, while the boys at Annandale, who were initially low on the variables, had a tendency to change upward.

Many of our "independent" variables are correlated with the initial level of protest or sympathy. Were we not to use regressed scores, most of the relationships would turn out in the wrong direction, as they did for Weeks. However, the use of regressed scores considerably reduces the variance of the change scores. In the case of protest change at Time Three, the variance was reduced by approximately 23 percent, thus decreasing the likelihood of getting large differences in any comparison. Therefore, we did not use the regressed scores when initial level of the dependent variable showed no correlations with the independent variable. In this latter case, regression toward the mean did not confound our findings.

FOOTNOTES

[1] Pearson's r.

[2] Quinn McNemar, Psychological Statistics (third edition; New York; John Wiley and Sons, 1962), p. 159.

[3] The use of randomly or systematically selected split-halfs would yield considerable sampling error, since the scale was only 15 items in length. To avoid this problem, we applied the Kuder-Richardson formula 20, using an analysis of variance method of computation described by Cyril Hoyt, "Test Reliability Obtained by Analysis of Variance," Psychometrika, VI, 153-160. Gulliksen points out that formula 20 is a lower boundary to the reliability coefficient (Harold Gulliksen, Theory of Mental Tests (New York: John Willey and Sons, 1950), p. 224).

[4] Ibid., pp. 159-160.

[5] See footnote 3.

[6] Pearson's r.

[7] These variances refer to the scores of the individuals remaining in the sample at Time Three. The standard deviations were 7.89 and 7.30, respectively. The difference between the two values was not due to a change in scale length--the scales were the same length--but probably a result of the higher drop-out rate among inmates with high protest scores.

[8] Due to rounding errors, the actual means were 3.89 and 24.97, respectively. "No change" in the case of regressed scores should be taken to mean that the person received a score equal to the mean. The regression adjustment eliminates any meaning with respect to the difference in actual scale scores. The mean protest and sympathy-reward scores for unregressed change are 26.5 and 4.26. The mean of 26.5 on protest indicates that there was an average increase of 1.5 points from Time One to Time Three. The mean of 4.26 on sympathy-reward change has no particular significance as an indicator of upward change for the total group as it is a combination of two separate change measures.

[9] Ashley Weeks, Youthful Offenders at Highfields (Ann Arbor, Michigan: University of Michigan Press, 1958).

[10] Ibid., pp. 118-128.

CHAPTER IX

ANALYSIS OF CHANGE: SOME SELECTED FINDINGS

PERSONALISM AND CHANGE

In Chapter VII, analysis of the relation between personalism, time served, and protest yielded the finding that personalistic inmates show a marked increase in protest over time. Time served, utilized to indicate the casual effect of time in the institution, raised a number of problems related to the selective characteristics of long-termers. Change over the time period of the panel, on the other hand, involves few of these problems. All inmates who were in the panel at the end were also in it at the beginning. Thus, all individuals analyzed had served an equal amount of time. Table XXIX shows the relationship between personalism and the two change measures, protest and sympathy; (for convenience, sympathy-reward change will be referred to as sympathy change). The means presented in the tables are for the unregressed change scores, since initial protest did not correlate with personalism.

Table XXIX

Relationship Between Personalism Level and Attitude Change

Personalism level	Mean protest change score	Mean sympathy change score	N
High (6-8)	28.3	3.08	26
Medium (4-5)	26.2	4.38	52
Low (0-3)	25.8	4.79	47

Probability that the protest means are drawn from a common population $> .05$. (F test, $F = 1.52$)

Probability that the sympathy means are drawn from a common population $< .01$. (F test, $F = 7.16$)

The data above are unregressed scores, measuring change from Time One to Time Three.

The relationship between personalism and sympathy change is especially striking. The obtained F is larger than for any other change relationship in the present study, as are the differences between the means.[1] Individuals who are low on personalism tend increasingly to come to believe that the staff is sympathetic and rewarding to inmates, whereas individuals who are high on personalism become increasingly convinced that the staff is unsympathetic and unrewarding. Compared to sympathy change, protest change shows a weaker relationship to personalism. This finding parallels the data in Chapter VII, where we found that for personalistic inmates time served was more strongly related to sympathy than to protest.

According to the data on time served, high personalism led to a decrease in sympathy and an increase in protest, while low personalism showed a weak tendency toward an increase in sympathy and a decrease in protest. Personalism has a more linear effect on sympathy change than on static sympathy; low personalism leads to increasing sympathy, and high personalism leads to decreasing sympathy. However, the relationship is somewhat more marked for those high on personalism as compared to those low on personalism. The data on personalism and protest are less than statistically significant; but if any conclusion is to be drawn, it is that high personalism leads to a change upward in protest, whereas low personalism is associated with a weak downward change in protest.

During the three-month time span of the panel, personalism scores tend to relate to sympathy in both upward and downward directions. The data on the effect of time served give us a way of looking at the effect of personalism over longer periods of time. In the long run, over one or two years of institutional experience, the major amount of change in sympathy is in the downward direction and occurs among inmates who are high on personalism. On the other hand, personalism does not have different effects on protest over the long, as compared to the short, run; for both time spans protest increases for those high on personalism and shows a weak decrease for those low on personalism.

The findings on personalism can now be tested in two ways, using static data and using change data. These two kinds of data are independent of one another, although they were obtained from the same respondents. There is no reason for similar results other than the validity of the basic hypothesis, since the time variables involved are completely different and the likelihood of two similar findings by statistical mischance is doubtless very low.

The question of causality may be raised at this point in the analysis. Can we argue that personalism causes change in sympathy?

One possibility that may be ruled out is a reverse causal relationship between personalism and sympathy. Personalism is a static variable; it is an average level of personalism. Thus, it cannot be argued that personalism is caused by sympathy change. On the other hand, it may be claimed that the correlation is spurious. Such an argument cannot be firmly rejected. It is possible that another variable, correlated with personalism, has a causal relation to sympathy change. Personalism, it might be argued, bears no causal relation to sympathy change. It correlated with the latter because of the correlation of personalism with another variable that causes change in sympathy.

No variable has been discovered that bears a higher relation to sympathy change than does personalism. This fact, plus the plausibility of the theoretical relation between personalism and sympathy change, leads us to conclude that a causal relation between the two variables is our best inference from the present data.

The possibility of mutual causality cannot be ruled out. In fact, personalism _change_ shows some correlation with sympathy change (Pearson's r = -.14). We may speculate about a sequence that begins with relatively high personalism, causing a decrease in sympathy, which causes a further increase in personalism. Such a sequence receives a bit of support from the observations of Kardiner and Ovesey in their work on the personality characteristics of Negroes.[2] Negroes, Kardiner and Ovesey claim, have a tendency to be suspicious and personalizing in their relations with others.[3] This is not surprising if one thinks about the position of the disprivileged minority in interracial conflict. The first question such a person is likely to ask himself when interacting with a member of the majority group may be, "What is _his_ attitude toward me?" The Negro lives in a white world characterized by negative sentiment directed toward himself, where any act that is less than completely negative is likely to be seen as having some unique, personal meaning. Of the 14 Negroes in our sample, 11 fell above the median on the distribution of personalism scores (Questionnaire One).[4] Thus, it may be argued that an individual who is involved in a negatively toned relationship with the world around him is likely to become increasingly personalistic in his orientation.

WORK CREW STATUS AND CHANGE

In Chapter VII no relationship was found between work crew status and protest. Table XXX presents data on work crew status and the protest and sympathy change measures for inmates whose status was unchanged during the time period covered.

A marked difference is seen between inmates low on status and the remaining inmates. The relationship is non-linear. Inmates high on status are not commensurately low on protest but are slightly higher than the middle group. If the high-status and middle-status groups are treated as one and compared with the low-status group, the probability of no difference is less than .05.

Awarding membership in a high-status work crew to an inmate does not produce accommodation. But awarding low status seems to yield an inmate who comes to perceive the staff as unsympathetic and who exhibits a distinct upswing in his level of protest. Data in Table XXXI on status change may provide some clue to this phenomenon.

Table XXX

Relationship Between Work Crew Status and Attitude Change for Those Whose Work Crew did not Change from Time One to Time Three

Work crew status	Mean protest change score	Mean sympathy change score	N
High	24.0	4.09	55
Medium	23.3	4.48	21
Low	27.6	3.55	11

Probability that the protest means are drawn from a common population > .05. (F test, F = 2.55)

Probability that the sympathy means are drawn from a common population > .05. (F test, F = 1.07)

The data above are regressed scores, measuring change from Time One to Time Three.

Table XXXI

Relationship Between Work Crew Status Change and Attitude Change

Work crew status change	Mean protest change score	Mean sympathy change score	N
Upward	26.6	3.14	22
Stable	24.2	4.11	90
Downward	27.2	3.62	13

Probability that the protest means are drawn from a common population < .05. (F test, F = 3.14)

Probability that the sympathy means are drawn from a common population < .05. (F test, F = 3.18)

Four individuals who were not assigned to work crews at the beginning of the period were classified as "upward" if they received assignment to a high-status work crew, downward if assigned to a low-status work crew, and stable if assigned to a middle-status work crew.

The attitude data above are regressed scores, measuring change from Time One to Time Three.

Inmates whose job status <u>increased</u> or <u>decreased</u> in the time period of the study showed an increase in protest and a decrease in sympathy. In other words, any change in status seems to result in an increasingly negative relationship with the staff. This seemingly anomalous finding has parallels in previous research. <u>The American Soldier</u>, for example, details such instances.[5] Men in the Military Police, where promotion was very slow, were less dissatisfied than men in the Air Force, where promotion was more rapid. College graduates received faster promotion but were more dissatisfied with promotional opportunities than were non-college graduates.[6] These findings are seen by Merton as relative deprivation fostered by reference group affiliation.[7] The Military Police are said to have experienced less relative deprivation because of their non-mobile reference group, while the college graduate experienced greater relative deprivation because of a relatively mobile reference group.

The military data did not relate changes in attitudes to changes in status. The use of the reference group concept in explaining the present data would seem problematic, unless it can be argued that the individual's friends are moving upward faster than he is. This plainly cannot be the case for our group of subjects; since our sample is biased in the pro-staff direction, it may even be that our sample received greater promotion than did their friends.

From the present point of view, a more plausible explanation is that, having been put in a position of greater relative dominance in the prison hierarchy, the upward mobile inmates became more <u>dominance-oriented,</u> i.e., more sensitized to the symbols of dominance, more "status conscious," more careful in scrutinizing their interactions with the staff for possibilities of negative exchange. The individual thus oriented is more likely to find instances of unfavorable exchanges that reduce his belief in the staff's sympathy and increase his level of protest.

The analysis that we are making could be stated in terms of the language of Merton, who argued that individuals, after becoming elevated in status, tend to experience an increase in aspirations which, in turn, create sensitivity to deprivations relative to those aspirations.[8] It seems unclear as to why aspirations should rise <u>faster</u> than opportunity. Our version of the argument may offer some help in solving the latter analytic difficulty. In effect, we point out that aspirations may not increase toward any specific goal; rather it may be that the upwardly mobile individual develops a heightened sensitivity to the <u>theme</u> of status and thereby becomes aware of a <u>new</u> set of opportunities to which he lacks access. The greater the importance of the status shift, the more the theme of status may tend to become a central part of the person's consciousness. Occupational status and its counterpart in increased or reduced privilege is likely to be of central importance to an inmate, as it is to a person in the free world outside the walls.

Those with stable high status tended to be only slightly higher on protest change than those with medium status, while those who experienced an increase in status moved markedly upward on protest. Taken together, the findings suggest that there may be a tendency for those who are upwardly mobile to move back toward the mean, after having arrived in their new jobs along with an increase in protest level. The downwardly mobile show no such movement toward the mean.

Objectively, the upwardly mobile inmate is receiving greater rewards than is the downwardly mobile inmate, and thus is experiencing a more favorable exchange than his less-fortunate counterpart (unless the increased status brings with it increased demands for conformity). Both types of inmates may tend to become dominance oriented, but it seems likely that in the long run the inmate with an objectively more favorable exchange will tend to be the less protesting of the two types.

Furthermore, it may be that as the change in job status loses its immediacy, it becomes less central to the self. Hence, the degree of dominance orientation may lesson. Fifty-five inmates held stable high status from Time One to Time Three. Estimating from our data on status change, approximately 10 of these 55 had moved up in the preceding three-month period. Thus the stable high-status inmates, not characterized by high protest, are largely those who had not recently acquired their status.

To summarize, the presence of objective threat to a balanced exchange is created for inmates who are low, or move down, in status. The granting of high status does not have the opposite effect. Such a finding gives little support to the notion that reward has a linear relation to conformity. In this prison setting the lack of rewards induces conflict, but in the short run the granting of high rewards has the same negative consequence.

THE SELECTIVITY OF REWARD

In Chapter VII, no correlation was found at Time One between protest and work crew status. This finding suggests the absence of selectivity by the staff in granting rewards. The data on change offer a test of this hypothesis. Table XXXII presents data on the relationship between protest and sympathy at the beginning of the period, and change in work crew status. It should indicate whether positive attitudes on the part of inmates evoke positive rewards from the staff in return.

Although the differences in protest are in the anticipated direction, they are so minute as possibly to have resulted from sampling variation. The sympathy scores show no consistent relationship to status change. These data would seem to indicate that work crew status is not used as a reward to inmates who hold positive attitudes.

There are numerous alternative explanations, however, for this finding. As was suggested earlier, the fact that status rewards and positive attitudes are unrelated may be a result of "therapeutic" standards that govern job assignment. Or the needs of specific work crews may be primary and a bureaucratic standard may operate. A third alternative might be that inmate preferences, functioning through informal inmate contacts with the work crew supervisor or other staff members, are the governing factors in work crew selection. If this were so, informal leadership might be the chief determinant of work crew status.

Whatever the reason for the findings of Table XXXII, they suggest something

Table XXXII

Relationship Between Work Crew Status Change and Initial
Protest and Sympathy Scores at Time One

Work crew status change (by Time Three)	Mean protest score (Time One)	Mean sympathy score (Time One)	N
Upward	24.1	16.7	22
Stable	25.3	17.3	90
Downward	25.5	15.4	13

Probability that the protest means are drawn from a common population $>.05$.
(F test, F = .20)

Probability that the sympathy means are drawn from a common population $>.05$.
(F test, F = .58)

See note on individuals unassigned to work crews in Table XXXI.

interesting when looked at from the inmate's point of view. The protesting inmate may not find that he is decreasing his opportunities by continuing his protest behavior, and the inmate who has a favorable view of staff attitudes may not receive reinforcement for this view from the kinds of job assignments he is given by the staff.

SELF-FRIENDS MATRIX AND CHANGE

In Chapter VII a technique was outlined for testing the audience-effect hypothesis. Self and friends were classified as to dominance orientation, and it was shown that the degree of dominance orientation of friends had relatively strong influence as compared to the dominance orientation of self. Table XXXIII reports the analysis for protest change rather than static protest. It should be noted that Table XXXIII is a test of the audience effect that is independent of the previous test (Tables XXIII and XXIV). The technique used for computing regressed protest change results in a correlation of zero between protest and protest change, subject to rounding errors. Thus there would seem to be no reason other than the validity of the hypothesis for a similarity between Tables XXXIII and XXIII

Findings of the two tests are exactly consistent. When both friends and self are dominance oriented, protest increases to the greatest degree; when neither friends nor self are dominance oriented, protest shows the maximum decrease. The intermediate cases are also parallel, with the friends' dominance orientation having a greater effect than the dominance orientation of self.

Table XXXIII

Relationship Between Self-Friends Matrix and Attitude Change

Type	Self orientation	Friends orientation	Mean protest change score	Mean sympathy change score	N
1	Dominance	Dominance	25.0	4.71	14
2	Non-dominance	Dominance	24.4	3.65	17
3	Dominance	Non-dominance	23.5	3.77	13
4	Non-dominance	Non-dominance	22.9	3.95	22

Probability that the protest means are drawn from a common population $>.05$.
(F test, F = .52)

Probability that the sympathy means are drawn from a common population $>.05$.
(F test, F = 1.18)

The data above are regressed scores, measuring change from Time One to Time Three.

The data on protest change in Table XXXIII are not statistically significant. The value of F for this relationship is below 1.00, indicating that the difference between the means could well occur by chance alone. This significance figure contrasts markedly with the differences between the means. The absolute differences between the means were relatively large, compared to the other relationships examined herein. It is likely that the small F is partly due to heterogeneity of variance between the cells. Cell four contains both square Johns and right guys, social types that have quite different means on the change variable. The pooling of dissimilar groups probably is responsible for the combined group having almost twice as high a variance as did the other groups in the matrix. Heterogeneity of variance is a liability of this type of analysis of friendship and can be compensated for by large samples.

Although neither of the independent tests of the audience effect yielded a significant F, the striking consistency between the tests encourages some confidence in both the stability and the theoretical meaning of the findings. We are led to conclude that individuals who have dominance-oriented friends, i.e., friends who are con politicians or outlaws, will have a tendency to be high on protest and to increase their protest scores. However, their <u>private views</u> of the staff will not reflect their expressed behavior, as measured by the protest scale. No consistent relationship is seen between the protest change means and the sympathy change means. Those who are highest on protest, Type 1 in the matrix, also show a marked increase in sympathy over the other types in the matrix.

Apparently, the dominance orientation of friends creates situations in which the inmate's relationship to the staff is one involving threat. The threat is not created by changing the inmate's view of the staff. Rather, it would seem that the threat is a result of the image that the inmate holds as to how his friends evaluate his interactions. The dominance-oriented group is likely to scrutinize his behavior for the possibility of unfavorable exchange relations with staff members. The threat is real and not psychological. Quietly the inmate in a dominance-oriented group can afford to harbor positive sentiments, but publicly he may not wish to express compliance.

INSTRUMENTALISM AND CHANGE

The instrumentalism scales measure the attitude of willingness to negotiate for reward. Instrumentalism bears no linear relationship to protest; the correlation between the two variables at Time One is -.04.[9] The lack of correlation is not surprising when it is remembered that the protesting right guys have low scores on the instrumentalism scale. Table XXXIV shows the relationships between instrumentalism and changes in protest scores.

The findings indicate the possibility of a curvilinear relationship between instrumentalism and protest change. While the differences are not statistically significant and will have to be viewed cautiously, the curvilinearity is relatively smooth. Protest scores decrease consistently from the low to the middle scores on instrumentalism, and then increase consistently.

Table XXXIV

Relationship Between Instrumentalism Score and Attitude Change

Instrumentalism score (Time One)	Mean protest change score	Mean sympathy change score	N
13 or greater	29.7	4.27	15
12	27.0	5.10	10
11	26.3	4.41	22
10	25.2	4.14	34
9	26.1	4.05	19
8 or less	26.7	4.12	25

The probability that the protest means are drawn from a common population $>$ .05. (F test, F = 1.14)

The probability that the sympathy means are drawn from a common population $>$ .05. (F test, F = .47)

The data above are unregressed scores, measuring change from Time One to Time Three.

Our original discussion of negotiated reward was couched in terms of styles of institutional life. In terms of the individual inmate, our hypothesis is that an orientation toward negotiated reward leads to dominance orientation and to threat. This hypothesis led to the prediction that the instrumentalism scale would be positively correlated with protest. Thus the present finding is unanticipated.

The nature of the scale itself suggests a partial interpretation of the curvilinear finding. Individuals who score high on the scale indicate that they will accommodate if given circumstances in which accommodation has a "payoff." The instrumental inmate has a good reason to accommodate--he wants something from the staff. Such an hypothesis receives some support from an earlier study by the author, in which a negative correlation was found between instrumentalism and protest for members of a political-religious organization.[10] Consider, on the other hand, the situation of the inmate with a very high instrumentalism score. It seems likely, given our present data, that he measures his success by his ability to gain privilege. Here our original argument regains its cogency; inmates when oriented toward negotiating privileges will experience high threat and become increasingly dominance oriented.

SOCIAL TYPE AND PROTEST

The attempt to make predictions about the change scores of the social types is difficult. Rather than attempt to do this, we shall present the data on the types and consider if our theory is relevant. Table XXXV presents data on change among the social types.

Table XXXV

Relationship Between Social Type at Time Two and Protest Change

Social type (Time Two)	Mean protest change score	N
Square John	23.1	35
Con politician	25.6	39
Outlaw	25.2	10
Right guy	25.2	26

The probability that the means are drawn from a common population $> .05$. (F test, F = 1.45)

Sixteen individuals could not be classified into any one of this type categories.

The data above are regressed scores, measuring change from Time One to Time Three.

The classification of inmates into the type categories was done on the basis of responses at Time Two, while change is for the period Time One to Time Three. Thus the types are based on self-concept items gathered in the mid-portion of the time period, whereas change is measured over the whole period.

Table XXXV indicates that change in the protest scores of right guys, outlaws, and con politicians are similar and in a slightly upward direction. Square Johns have a relatively marked tendency to move downward in protest. For purposes of the present analysis we shall compare mainly the square Johns and politicians.

Schrag describes the square Johns and the con politicians in terms suggesting that these individuals tend to be accommodating inmates. "(The politician) may write speeches and letters for the warden, prepare institutional publicity and propaganda or organize radio skits for presentation."[11] The case history materials on these inmates described them as "well-behaved."[12] Nonetheless, our data indicate that the con politician's protest score tends to be relatively high, and to remain high or move slightly upward. On the other hand, the square John is low in protest and has a tendency to move downward.

In summarizing the findings of numerous studies, Schrag points out that square Johns show strong guilt for their offenses and expect to pay for their crimes in order to return to civilian life with a clean slate.[13] Given the foregoing, when a staff member makes demands for conformity on a square John, it seems likely that the demands will not be seen as an assertion of the staff's dominance. First, the square John tends not to be dominance oriented, as was indicated in the analysis of the instrumentalism scale. Second, the demands are likely to be seen as a reflection of society's values, rather than of the staff member's attitude toward the inmates.

The con politician, as we have shown, is relatively high in dominance orientation and is likely to see demands as a reflection of the staff member's attitude. Square Johns are likely to be concerned with supporting societal values. Con politicians, high on personalism, are typically oriented toward circumventing the norms and proving that personal attitudes govern norm enforcement.

Thus an objective loss of privilege is likely to be experienced as an attack by the politician and is likely to have degrading implications, which it would not have for the square John. The con politician may be successful in manipulating the staff and evading the rules. However, he is so highly focused on the theme of manipulation and rule evasion that "trouble" is likely to come his way. Schrag's work suggests that many politicians have an "in" with the staff,[14] but the "in" is likely to be tenuous because of the politician's constant involvement in unsavory dealings.

An outlaw's comment suggests an important distinction between con politicians and square Johns: "Sometimes the politicians get too chummy with the bulls (guards), but more often they get what they are after. There is nothing wrong with that. It's just being smart."[15] The square John may not wish to "be smart" or to be seen by others in those terms. If he is so oriented, he will experience less threat initially and as his prison career wears on. In contrast, the outlaw type echoes the concern of the con politician with privilege and the maintenance of favorable exchanges with the staff. Like the con politician, the outlaw's protest level increases over time.

Table XXXVI shows data on the social types and protest change, based on type classification at Time Three. At Time Three there were fewer square Johns than at Time Two. This finding is consistent with Schrag's statement that square Johns rapidly move into other categories as prison experience is acquired. Table XXXVI indicates that those remaining in the category have an even greater tendency to move downward in protest than did those who were square Johns at Time Two.

Table XXXVI

Relationship Between Social Type at Time Three and Protest Change

Social Type (Time Three)	Mean protest change score	N
Square John	21.7	23
Con politicians	25.7	43
Outlaw	26.0	7
Right guy	25.4	36

Probability that the means are drawn from a common population $<$ .05. (F test, F = 3.43)

Fourteen individuals could not be classified into any one of the type categories.

The data above are regressed scores, measuring change from Time One to Time Three.

FOOTNOTES

[1] The statement about the significance of the difference between the means is true for both the regressed change scores and the unregressed scores.

[2] Abraham Kardiner and Lionel Ovesey, *The Mark of Oppression* (New York: W.W. Norton and Co., 1951).

[3] Ibid., p. 308.

[4] Nonetheless, the Negroes tend to have low protest scores. Actually, the use of the word "conflict" in describing Negro-white relations is not consistent with our definition of the term. Traditionally, Negroes have not expressed, in behavior, the negative sentiments that are often felt toward whites. The terms "tension" or alienation would be more appropriate than "conflict" in this case. A particularly intriguing possibility is that the personalism that is generated in Negro-white relations becomes

generalized to intra-group attitudes of Negroes. Of Negro voluntary associations, Kardiner and Ovesey state, "There is continuous discord, jockeying for position and prestige and insistence that each member must have his own way." Such a picture is consistent with our own characterization of the personalistic individual as one who sees the demands of others as attacks upon himself. In the Negro world, interpersonal alienation seems to find the expression that is inhibited in Negro-white relations.

[5] Samuel Stouffer, et al., The American Soldier (Princeton, N.J.: Princeton University Press, 1949), Vol. I.

[6] Ibid., pp. 250-258.

[7] Robert K. Merton, Social Theory and Social Structure (revised edition; Glencoe, Ill.: The Free Press, 1957), Chapter 8.

[8] Ibid., p. 136.

[9] Pearson's r.

[10] George S. Rothbart, "Ideology and Strategy: A Study of Attitudes toward the Organizational Process" (unpublished Master's thesis, University of Washington, Seattle, 1962), pp. 135-148.

[11] Clarence C. Schrag, "Social Types in a Prison Community" (unpublished Master's thesis, University of Washington, Seattle, 1944), p. 77.

[12] Ibid., p. 82.

[13] Clarence C. Schrag, "Some Foundations for a Theory of Corrections" in Donald R. Cressey (ed.), The Prison (New York: Holt, Rinehart, and Winston, Inc., 1961), p. 348.

[14] Schrag, "Social Types in a Prison Community," op. cit., p. 75.

[15] Ibid., p. 78.

CHAPTER X

ANALYSIS OF CHANGE: EXCHANGE BALANCE

THEORIES OF EXCHANGE BALANCE

In Chapter VI we reported that sympathy and reward were negatively correlated with protest. While this finding was consistent with theoretical expectations, it may not be completely explained by the theory developed here. The theory states that an unfavorable exchange of values will be perceived as status degradation and will thus be threatening to the inmate. Threat, in turn, will lead to protest. The theory offers a clear explanation of why individuals who are low on protest and low on sympathy will move to a state of high protest. Such individuals perceive staff demands as unreciprocated, i.e., the staff is willing to give little in exchange for the multitude of demands it makes upon the inmates.

The other end of the scale--the cases of individuals high on protest and high on sympathy--is more difficult to cope with. Why should such individuals move toward a lesser degree of protest? Their present situation is not status degrading; in fact, the staff is degrading in their eyes. The "status threat" hypothesis predicts that no change will occur in these cases. What we shall call a "favorable exchange" should not be stressful for the inmates, if the status threat hypothesis is valid.

A number of current theoretical formulations make a contrasting prediction to that of the status threat hypothesis. They predict that the case in which the inmate is receiving a favorable exchange in his relationships to the staff is *not* a stable state. A review of three of these formulations may help in interpreting the data on consistency and inconsistency between protest and sympathy.

THREE ALTERNATIVE HYPOTHESES

1. <u>A favorable perception of staff attitudes induces conformity.</u>

There are two alternative versions of this proposition, both of which have some vogue in the thinking of social scientists. The first stresses the pull of a positive affective response directed to ego by alter. It might be called a theory of gratitude, i.e., ego likes to be nice to alters who are nice to him. The second alternative

-116-

emphasizes the reasons for ego's positive picture of alter. In the case of the prison, the favorable image might be generated by a staff that is willing to offer inducements for conformity, at least to ego. It is these inducements, rather than the pull of a positive affective response, that induces compliant behavior.

Our data thus far offer little support for the view that positive responses from alter induce conformity. A change to higher job status tends to increase protest. The inmate who is low on personalism tends to acquire an increasingly favorable view of the staff in the short run, but the change in sympathy does not produce a commensurate decrease in protest.

2. <u>A favorable exchange state causes guilt.</u>

Both Homans[1] and Gouldner[2] claim that social relations are generally governed by a norm which states that "each person should give as much as he gets." Gouldner calls this the "norm of reciprocity," while Homans labels it "the rule of distributive justice." Gouldner notes exceptions in the cases of children and some others.

3. <u>The overly favorable exchange state changes with the staff's interaction with the inmate.</u>

By combining the status threat proposition developed in this research with a concern for the objective consequences of the inmate's actions, what we may call an <u>interaction</u> theory of threat may be developed. It holds that a favorable exchange from the point of view of the inmate is an unfavorable exchange to the staff member. Under these conditions the staff members is likely to make a hostile response to the inmate, thereby initiating a cycle of interaction that results in a marked change in the inmate's perception of the staff.

While such an argument is plausible, some of our data on the response the staff makes to protesting inmates does not support it. It was noted that high job status was not differentially given to inmates with low protest scores. Of course, the data relates to only one objective consequence of protest. However, it is the writer's impression that the willingness of the Reformatory staff to tolerate misconduct is relatively high. Especially among the treatment staff, hostility from inmates is viewed as a result of their characteristic "problems" of adjustment in the world. Many members of the Reformatory staff feel that a "firm" but understanding and non-hostile attitude is what is needed to provide help with problems of adjustment. Seemingly, the staff has a higher willingness to tolerate an exchange imbalance than do the inmates.

Western State Reformatory is a treatment-oriented institution. Over the years of the present warden's tenure, selection procedures and staff training programs have produced a relatively treatment-oriented custody staff. Nonetheless, custodial officers are likely to be less permissive of misconduct than are members of the treatment staff. As we have seen, it is the custodial officers who are the important objects of protest, but they are not responsible for making job assignments. Hence, the data on job status may overdraw a picture of staff tolerance. Indeed, the data on protest and rule violations made a strong case for the proposition that protesting inmates are likely to evoke a punitive response from the staff.

A phenomenological version of the above theory is possible. Inmates who see themselves as protesting may project their own responses onto the staff members. Since they might respond to their own hostile behavior quite negatively, were they staff members, they may fail to recognize certain patterns of tolerance among staff members. Many inmates do, indeed, have very punitive beliefs about the handling of misbehavior. While going unsung in the inmate ideology of contempt for the staff, these punitive beliefs may influence the inmate's projections about a relatively tolerant staff. Of course, some inmates have a well-developed capacity, sharpened by long years of commitment, for recognizing patterns of staff tolerance. Such inmates are likely to explore the tolerance limits with a view toward finding out the extent of misbehavior a staff member will permit before changing his view of the inmates.

The above theories suggest that the sympathy-protest relation may be viewed as a balanced state and that unbalanced states will tend to move toward balance.

A TEST OF THE EXCHANGE BALANCE HYPOTHESIS

In order to test the balance theory, all possible combinations of protest and sympathy were listed. They are as follows:

1. High protest, low sympathy.
2. Medium protest, medium sympathy.
3. Low protest, high sympathy.
4. High protest, high sympathy.
5. High protest, medium sympathy.
6. Medium protest, high sympathy.
7. Medium protest, low sympathy.
8. Low protest, low sympathy.
9. Low protest, medium sympathy.

The first three combinations are considered as balanced states. In the second set of three combinations, ego sees himself as giving less than he is receiving. In the last three combinations, ego perceives that he gives more than he receives. According to the theory, the balanced pairs (1, 2, and 3) will produce no change in protest or sympathy level. Pairs 4, 5, and 6 can be returned to balance by a downward change in either sympathy or protest. We call these the "downward" pairs. Pairs 7, 8, and 9 can be returned to balance by an upward change in either protest or sympathy. These are called "upward" pairs.

In following the analysis of exchange imbalance, it is crucial to remember that protest and sympathy are negatively correlated. Hence a return to balance can be accomplished by moving in the same direction on both variables, not by moving in different directions. An individual who is high on both variables is out of balance and can become balanced by moving downward to a medium score on both variables or to a low score on either one of the variables. The empirical classification of the pairs was made by subdividing sympathy and protest into tertiles. For the cutting points, see Appendix C.

Table XXXVII summarizes the data on the relation of balance and imbalance to sympathy and protest change. The balance predictions are all confirmed by Table XXXVII. In the balanced pairs, protest shows only a little change, and sympathy shows no change at all. "Upward" pairs show upward change in both protest and sympathy. "Downward" pairs show downward change in both variables. Two points are worthy of special attention in this connection. First, the amount of change is relatively small, compared to some of our previous findings. Second, the magnitude of the change varies with the type of imbalance.

Table XXXVII

Relationship Between Protest-Sympathy Combinations
and Attitude Change

Protest-sympathy combination	Mean protest change score	Deviation from total group mean	Mean sympathy change score	Deviation from total group mean	N
Unbalanced - upward	26.16	+1.19	4.24	+.35	25
Balanced	24.69	- .28	3.89	.00	74
Unbalanced - downward	24.62	- .35	3.54	-.35	26
Total group mean	24.97		3.89		

The probability that the protest means are drawn from a common population $>.05$. (F test, F = .76)

The probability that the sympathy means are drawn from a common population $>.05$. (F test, F = 1.08)

The above data are regressed scores, measuring change from Time One to Time Three.

THE LIMITED EFFECT OF EXCHANGE IMBALANCE

Exchange balance or imbalance is a relationship between perception of self and perception of others. Thus it is an example of cognitive balance. The concept of cognitive balance has been used with considerable success by a number of researchers, among them Newcomb,[3] Festinger,[4] Brehm,[5] and Osgood,[6] and in the theoretical work of Heider.[7]

Some of the studies cited have shown large changes in cognition as a result of unbalanced states. It is therefore surprising that our results are relatively weak, especially considering that the cognitive variables are highly correlated in the static state. There is one important difference, however, between the present study and the psychological research cited above. Most of the latter studies are experimental, using some kind of laboratory stimulus and touching on relatively peripheral attitudes. Newcomb's study is an exception to this rule. He analyzed the response of college students to friends in a situation in which most of the friends had been recently acquired. In all of the studies a novel stimulus appeared in the cognitive environment and was likely to introduce marked change into the subjects' perceptions.

In the present study inmates were not introduced to a novel setting. The weakness of the present findings can be partly understood by asking, "In the cognitively stable environment of the prison, why are some subjects in a state of imbalance?" Two answers can be given to this question. First, the out-of-balance subjects may have recently experienced radical cognitive stimuli, such as changed custody status, new jobs, or important changes in parole status. Second, the out-of-balance subjects may have developed mechanisms for maintaining imbalance, i.e., imbalance may be a normal state for them. While in the long run these subjects may return to a balanced state, the process may be a very slow one.

The small changes induced by cognitive imbalance result in statistically weak findings. The findings are crucial, however, and we shall accept them for just what they are--our best estimate as to the relationship between cognitive balance and change in protest and perceptions of staff attitudes.

CHANGES RELATED TO EXCHANGE IMBALANCE

Table XXXVII indicates that protest change does not show the same relationship to exchange imbalance as does sympathy. Sympathy change shows an approximately linear relationship to imbalance. The upward pairs show a deviation of .35 from the overall mean, and the downward pairs show a deviation of -.35 (the exact numerical correspondence should not be taken too seriously).

Contrasted to sympathy change, protest change scores show a different kind of relationship to exchange imbalance. The downward pairs deviate only -.35 on protest, in contrast to a +1.19 deviation for the upward pairs. Furthermore, the downward pairs show differences in protest of only -.07 from the balanced pairs.

Our data suggests that imbalance induces a change in the perception of the staff in a downward or upward direction, whichever will tend to return the person to a balanced state. But imbalance does not produce sizeable downward changes in protest. In the case of high protest and high sympathy, for example, balance is likely to be achieved by a reduction of sympathy. In the opposite case, low protest and low sympathy, the balance is likely to be achieved by a combination of upward changes in both protest and sympathy. In an important way these findings are consonant with the data on personalism and on work crew status which suggested that the effect of these variables was non-linear. Low status and high personalism were related to an <u>increase</u> in protest, but having a "favorable" score on these variables did not relate to a decrease in protest.

The downward pairs move downward only on sympathy, not on protest. Therefore, in order to return to a balanced state, the sympathy scores ought to show a greater magnitude of change than the upward pairs. The upward pairs are "getting help" from protest in returning to balance, but the downward pairs are getting little such help. No difference is observed between the magnitudes of sympathy change for the upward and downward pairs. <u>This finding implies that downward pairs may have a lesser tendency to return to balance.</u>

These findings also offer support for the hypothesis about the status meanings of an exchange imbalance. That hypothesis implies that a more salient stress exists for an individual in an unfavorable exchange than in a favorable exchange. The notions of Homans and Gouldner are only partly consistent with the data. If it works at all, the "norm of reciprocity" appears to work primarily on ego's cognitions of others, when it is ego himself who is its violator. The mechanism seen here strongly smacks of a "technique of neutralization."[8] Homans recognized this possibility when he said:

> Distributive justice may . . . fail . . . to a man's advantage rather than to his disadvantage, and then he may feel guilty rather than angry; he has done better for himself than he ought to have done. But he is less likely to make a prominent display of guilt than of his anger. Indeed a man in this happy situation is apt to find arguments convincing to himself that the exchange is not really to his advantage after all.[9]

Acknowledging an exception to an argument does not explain the exception. It is not clear from Homan's argument why the guilt influences only cognition, whereas anger at being unjustly deprived does have an influence on behavior. Our argument stresses the element of status degradation and does explain why less stress to change behavior is felt in the above instance.

The data are least consistent with the theory that a favorable view of staff attitudes will induce compliant behavior. Viewing staff attitudes as more positive than is ego's behavior appears to induce a change in the view of the staff and not a change in behavior.

Figure 3 shows the scatter plot between protest and sympathy at Time One. Inspection of the deviations from the regression line does not show any striking tendency for an accumulation of high-protest, high-sympathy inmates. The absence of curvilinearity would seem to indicate that downward sympathy change accomplished the job of returning the individual to a balanced state.

A CONCLUSION

Our theory, stressing status threat, does not, by itself, explain why sympathy moves downward in the case of a favorable exchange. Homans and Gouldner can readily explain why sympathy moves downward in that instance, but can explain neither why <u>only</u> sympathy changes nor why favorable exchange does not return to

FIGURE 3

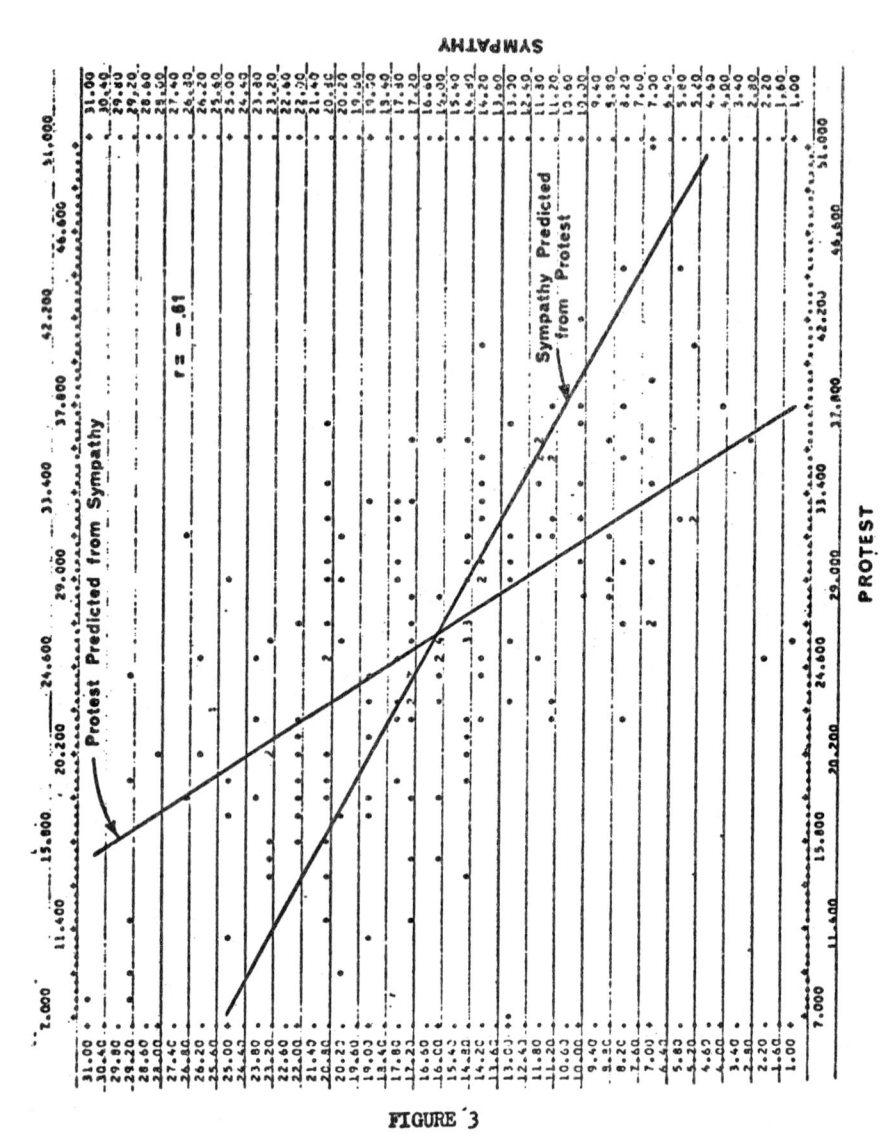

PROTEST VERSUS SYMPATHY SCATTERGRAM

-122-

balance to the same degree, or at the same rate, as the unfavorable exchange. Homans might suggest that individuals wish to maximize their "profits" as long as they can minimize their guilt. They can do this by maintaining a slight balance of "get" over "give"; that was the view implicit in the example Homans offered. But protest is not "good" in the sense that trading an apple core for the arduous task of whitewashing a fence is "good." What does an individual gain by protest?

The interaction theory cited earlier can be utilized to provide help in explaining the favorable exchange. Imagine the case of the individual who sees the staff as highly sympathetic, but sees himself as behaving in a pretesting manner toward staff persons (and probably is correct in his self judgment according to the data of Chapter V). He lives his life in the harsh, degrading environment that characterizes even the treatment-oriented prison that we are describing. Maintenance of a favorable exchange helps heal some of these pains of imprisonment.

The realities of his interpersonal relations may not permit the above inmate to easily maintain his positive view of the staff and thus to maintain a favorable exchange. While it is likely that staff members have considerable tolerance for misconduct, the data of Chapter V strongly indicate that the staff, especially custodial officers, are likely to begin displaying a negative response when the inmate's behavior begins to appear consistently less compliant than the behavior of most other inmates. Homans and Gouldner suggest that under these conditions the inmate will experience guilt.

The highly protesting inmate with a view of the staff as highly sympathetic is involved in a favorable exchange relationship, compared to other inmates. But the relationship to staff is likely to be in the process of becoming _less_ favorable. Under these conditions the balance theory of Gouldner and Homans predicts that both protest and sympathy will diminish.

The predictions of the status threat hypothesis are in strong contrast to the predictions of balance theory. The status threat hypothesis predicts that behavior and cognitions will not diminish at the same time. The experiential world of the high-protest, high-sympathy inmate is one in which the exchanges are becoming less and less favorable to the inmate. Under these conditions it is unlikely that he will become less protesting because such a response would only further reduce the favorability of his exchanges.

In contrast, the data indicate that the inmate with an _unfavorable_ exchange becomes more protesting and comes to view the staff as more sympathetic. He has every reason to be willing to see the staff as responding more favorably to him. Since the inmate's behavior is becoming increasingly protesting, a more favorable view of the staff increases the favorability of the exchange relationship, when viewed from his vantage point. Such an inmate is changing his behavior in a manner _consistent_ with his changing view of the staff.

The status threat hypothesis predicts that sympathy and protest may increase together but will not diminish together. Thus it seems highly consistent with the findings at hand.

FOOTNOTES

[1] George C. Homans, <u>Social Behavior: Its Elementary Forms</u> (New York: Harcourt, Brace, and World, Inc., 1961).

[2] Alvin W. Gouldner, "The Norm of Reciprocity: A Preliminary Statement," <u>American Sociological Review</u>, XXV (April, 1960), 161-178.

[3] Theodore M. Newcomb, <u>The Acquaintance Process</u> (New York: Holt, Rinehart, and Winston, Inc., 1961).

[4] Leon Festinger, <u>A Theory of Cognitive Dissonance</u> (Evanston, Ill.: Row, Peterson, 1957); "Cognitive Consequences of Forced Compliance," <u>Journal of Abnormal and Social Psychology,</u> LVIII (March, 1959), 203-210.

[5] Jack W. Brehm and Arthur R. Cohen, <u>Explorations in Cognitive Dissonance</u> (New York: John Wiley and Sons, Inc., 1962).

[6] Charles E. Osgood and Percy H. Tannenbaum, "The Principle of Contruity in the prediction of Attitude Change," <u>Psychological Review</u>, L (January, 1955), 349-353.

[7] Fritz Heider, <u>The Psychology of Interpersonal Relations</u> (New York: John Wiley and Sons, Inc., 1958).

[8] Gresham M. Sykes and David Matza, "Techniques of Neutralization; A Theory of Delinquency," <u>American Sociological Review,</u> XXII (December, 1957), 664-670.

[9] Homans, op. cit., pp. 75-76.

CHAPTER XI

AN EXPLORATORY EXPERIMENT

In the last chapter it was suggested that one factor inhibiting effective research on cognitive processes among inmates is the relative lack of novel stimuli in the prison population. Novel stimuli may be required to upset cognitive balance and to facilitate attitude change. A change in job status seems to be such a stimulus. Other events that might have an impact on the inmate's view of the staff are a large reduction in the inmate's sentence by the parole board, a sentence to solitary confinement, or an unexpected liberalization of privileges (privileges are frequently increased after the inmate has served a few months time). Except for changes in work crew status, most of these events occur infrequently. Hence, insufficient cases preclude detailed analysis. Furthermore, the inmate culture may so reinterpret the effects of these events that they are not likely to have much impact on behavior. This is not to say that these stimuli lack importance. Rather, it is to suggest that many stimuli do not vary enough to be studied in our population.

An experiment may provide a way of introducing larger changes in cognitive stimuli than occur under normal conditions. With this hope in mind, we attempted to work out techniques for manipulating two stimulus variables, sympathy and personalism, and to observe any consequent changes in protest. The experiment was planned in the "classical" framework of random assignment of subjects, but, as we shall see, it did not work out that way. While the classical design was not achieved, the findings may nevertheless provide an opportunity to study cognitive changes in a novel setting unlike that which is usual in prison.

A further value of the experiment lies in its affording a better understanding of the processes by which personalism and sympathy undergo change. In the attempt to manipulate stimuli designed to produce change in protest, we may be able to find out something about the stimuli themselves.

We shall call the experiment dealing with protest, personalism, and sympathy the "feedback" treatment, because its purpose was to provide to the inmates reliable information about prison life. During the same period, Dr. Herbert Costner[1] carried out an experiment designed to change inmate role performance. We shall refer to that experiment as the "co-optation" treatment. Dr. Costner was interested in a dependent variable that was different from ours, and his results will be fully reported elsewhere. However, we shall look at the personalsim, sympathy, and protest scores of his subjects in order to gain some additional insight into our own research.[2]

THE EXPERIMENTAL DESIGN

In the experiment, we planned to have three groups of subjects. Inmates were randomly drawn from those in the panel at Time One and were randomly assigned to one of three groups. One group was assigned to the feedback treatment, another to the co-optation treatment, and the third served as a control. The inmates selected were then notified of their selection and told when and where they were to participate in the experiment. All inmates had been previously informed that the sessions would be held one night a week for four weeks. They also know that they would be paid a dollar for their participation. A dollar was a small sum and we were careful to point out that it was not as much as we would have liked.[3]

The rate of non-participation came as something of a shock to us. Of the 170 inmates who were in the panel at Time One, 110 were eventually assigned to either the co-optation or the feedback treatment groups. Only 60 of the 110, or 55 percent, attended at least one session. Having attended one session, the inmates had a strong tendency to drop out. For example, in the feedback experiment 61 percent of the inmates dropped out before attending a third session. Whatever the reason for the dropout, it makes the interpretation of the experiment far more problematic than in an experiment in which one is able to maintain random assignment.

The main effect of non-participation was to make the sample highly selective with regard to some of the variables we wished to examine. In the case of protest, in particular, non-participation severely limited the range of the scores of the experimental subjects. The non-participation rate of the low-protest quartile was 44 percent, in contrast to a 73 percent non-participation rate for the high-protest quartile. The low rate of participation forced us to re-evaluate our intention of utilizing a complex research design.

MANIPULATION OF THE STIMULUS VARIABLES

The purpose of the feedback treatment was to affect personalism, sympathy, and, in consequence, protest. To do this, a simple mechanism was employed. Information was provided to the inmates from sociological studies of prison life. A number of studies had been done at this Reformatory. Materials from those studies were combined with other findings about the attitudes of staff members and of inmates and the reasons for their attitudes. Information of the following kinds were stressed:

1. Evidence was presented that inmate and staff opinions on many issues are more similar than would appear on the surface. Stress was placed on misinformation contained in common-sense notions about staff members and inmates. The purpose was to (a) increase sympathy for the staff

and (b) decrease the influence of the public, anti-staff inmate culture.

2. Inmates were motivated to examine objectively the various kinds of situational pressures that they experience in their social worlds. Routine problems of prison life were carefully examined by group discussion methods.

To provide the first kind of information, heavy reliance was placed on Wheeler's study of this particular reformatory.[4] Information so close to home should have a high level of natural interest to these inmates. The second kind of information was provided by a series of discussions of various sociological research findings concerning prisons and other formal organizations.

The co-optation experiment involved the inmate in a series of discussions with the "fish" (newly admitted inmates) from the reception and guidance unit. The more experienced inmates were expected to inform the "fish" about prison life so as to make their adjustment easier when they were released into the main prison population. What was said in these sessions was completely the responsibility of the five to ten inmates from our panel who made up each group of inmate "advisors." By placing the inmate advisors in a pro-social role, it was hoped to co-opt them into the legitimate system and thus influence their self-conceptions.

THE EXPERIMENTAL RESULTS

There was considerable interest in the feedback information among many of the inmate respondents. A few found it boring. The discussions were conducted in a relatively permissive atmosphere which allowed such expression of feeling. Under these conditions the inmates at first spent a good deal of time attacking the research. Especially in the case of Wheeler's findings on inmate misperceptions, considerable denial was expressed. As the sessions continued, however, the findings began to make more sense to the inmates. It is the author's impression that the information on inmate life was particularly intriguing to the inmates. The discussion of social types, prison argot, and leadership proved exciting and the research findings were readily absorbed. But when it came to descriptions of the staff world, the inmates' perceptions were so strongly established that changes in their cognitive systems were difficult to achieve. Many of the inmates took pride in their expert knowledge of the criminal or inmate world. They were happy to receive new information and to provide their own insights in return. They seemed to have far less interest in information and understanding about the staff's role in prison life.

In the co-optation experiment, high interest was generated, but also some suspicion. Much to the surprise of some staff members, the inmates did not use the opportunity to express extensive anti-staff sentiment. On the contrary, they often expressed some appreciation of the fairness of the staff. This was noticeable even in inmates who had expressed considerable anti-staff sentiment in the feedback experiment.

Table XXXVIII provides information on the relation of the co-optation and feedback treatments to protest and sympathy change. A small group of subjects participated in both treatments. The control group consisted of inmates who were not assigned to any treatment sessions, while the drop-out group included inmates who attended one or two sessions but dropped out before the third session.

According to the evidence, the impact of the treatments on sympathy change is virtually nil. The group that participated in the feedback treatment shows slightly more downward change in sympathy than does the control group. The co-optation treatment group shows results that are about the same as the control group. Only the drop-outs show any sympathy change, and that is in a marked downward direction. Dropping out is strongly related to holding an increasingly unfavorable perception of staff attitudes.

However, the relationship of the treatments to protest is more in accord with our expectations. All three treatment groups change downward in their level of protest. By contrast, the control group and the drop-out group show an increase in protest. The strongest downward shift is among the co-optation subjects. Most of the differences, however, are relatively small. Findings for the feedback group are equivocal except for those subjects who completed the treatment program. If the subjects who completed only two sessions are included, the mean for the feedback group is 24.5--higher than any mean except that of the drop-out group. Thus, in the feedback group, the reduction of protest may be a function of selectivity and not of the presumed stimulus.

Table XXXVIII

The Relationship of Experimental Groups to
Protest and Sympathy Change

Experimental group	Mean protest change score	Mean sympathy change score	N
Co-optation	22.5	4.45	11
Combined co-optation and feedback	23.3	3.83	6
Feedback	24.4	4.20	20
Control	25.1	4.42	43
Drop-out	25.7	3.20	20

Probability that the protest means are drawn from a common population $>$ .05.
(F test, F = 1.21)

Probability that the sympathy means are drawn from a common population $>$ .05.
(F test, F = 2.07)

The above data are regressed scores, measuring change from Time One to Time Three.

If the feedback treatment did not successfully change protest or sympathy, did it reduce personalism? Table XXXIX presents the data on personalism change and also on initial personalism. The data suggest that the feedback treatment had the effect of raising rather than of lowering personalism.

A number of things are of interest in Table XXXIX. First, the drop-outs have the highest rate of upward movement in the table. Second, the drop-outs have a markedly higher initial level of personalism than do the control and treatment groups in the table. Third, the group receiving the co-optation treatment shows more downward movement on personalism than does the feedback group.

The drop-outs are high on initial personalism and are more personalistic at the end of the period than at the beginning. They also move strongly downward in their level of sympathy. It is possible that the treatment was threatening to what may be a balanced cognitive state. Thus they remove themselves from a disturbing stimulus.

Table XXXIX

Relationship of Experimental Groups to Personalism
and Personalism Change

Experimental group	Mean personalism score	Mean personalism change score	N
Co-optation	4.09	3.64	11
Combined co-optation and feedback	2.71	3.00	6
Feedback	4.10	4.10	20
Control	3.68	3.68	43
Drop-out	4.75	4.20	20

Probability that the personalism means are drawn from a common population $<.05$. (F test, F = 2.77)

Probability that personalism change means are drawn from a common population is $>.05$. (F test, F = .89)

Personalism change is an unregressed score, measuring change from Time One to Time Two.

In general, then, the co-optation method seems effective in reducing the protesting attitude of many inmates and also in reducing their tendency to view events in a personalistic manner. The feedback method, while it may have some slight effect on protest, does not seem to influence sympathy, and it may have an effect on personalism which is the reverse of that intended. Neither method seems effective in increasing the level of sympathy. One possible explanation for the weak influence on sympathy is that the "outsiders" who handled the treatment programs were university professors and students who had no official role in the management of the prison. If the program had any effect on the inmates' attitudes toward the persons who managed the treatment program, this is not reflected in their attitudes toward the prison's staff. By contrast, protest, a more general orientation toward action, seems to have been affected by both treatment methods.

A stronger finding is that inmates who are high on protest and personalism and low on sympathy tend to deal with the experimental stimulus by withdrawing. The drop-outs, in addition, show an increase in protest and personalism and a decrease in sympathy over the time period covered by the study. Their cognitive systems apparently were balanced at the beginning of the study, and by rejecting the disturbing experimental stimulus they were able to maintain or to strengthen the original attitude-set. Rejection of the experimental stimulus means that for these inmates our attempt to introduce a novel stimulus was probably a failure.

FOOTNOTES

[1] Assistant Professor, Department of Sociology, University of Washington, Seattle.

[2] Very grateful acknowledgement is made to Dr. Costner for permission to use the fruits of his labor.

[3] Research on cognitive balance suggests that minimal rewards are, under certain conditions, more effective than large rewards.

[4] Stanton Wheeler, "Social Organization in a Correctional Community" (unpublished Ph.D. dissertation, University of Washington, Seattle, 1958).

CHAPTER XII

SUMMARY AND CONCLUSIONS

THE PROPOSITIONS

This study began with the development of a series of propositions about conflict behavior. The twelve main propositions of the theory are reviewed below.

1. Conflict is likely to involve interaction between two parties which is narrowly focused on the question of which party is the dominant one. In a conflict state, every interaction is likely to be evaluated for its symbolic meaning in settling the question of dominance.

A series of propositions was generated in an attempt to specify the conditions under which a dominance-centered relationship arises. Let us restate them here in terms that are appropriate to the social-psychological data of this study.

2. Conflict tends to be a mutually reinforcing relationship. Parties in conflict react to each other in a way that intensifies the conflict, rather than reduces it. If reinforcement does not occur, the conflict will dissipate.

3. If any of the parties to an interaction evaluate the interaction in terms of its effects on dominance relations, conflict is likely to occur. When one of the parties is not hostile toward the other, he is likely to become so if the other party views interaction in dominance terms.

4. Strong threats to the self-esteem, especially in terms of conception of self as autonomous and powerful, will tend to produce movement into the dominance dimension.

5. An unbalanced exchange relationship is a symbol of the dominance of the party who gets more than he gives. Unbalanced exchange threatens self-esteem of the disfavored party and produces movement onto the dominance dimension.

6. If the self, or a party external to the interaction in question, or an external event is seen as the source of the demands on oneself, the transaction is not viewed as an exchange and thus it loses its meaning as an assertion of dominance.

7. An orientation toward negotiating for reward reinforces the tendency to conceptualize interaction in terms of dominance.

8. An orientation toward negotiating for reward tends to threaten the actor's (inmate's) self-esteem and thus it encourages him to counterattack.

A series of less-formal propositions were evolved about the effects of the interpersonal milieu.

9. Culture (e.g., norms supporting staff-inmate opposition) increases the likelihood that an inmate will see staff demands as different from his own, thereby creating a more unfavorable exchange relationship for the inmate.

10. The milieu may provide the inmate with a negative picture of the staff's attitude toward inmates, thereby decreasing the favorableness of the exchange for the inmate.

11. The milieu may scrutinize the inmate's interaction with the staff, paying attention to the existence of unfavorable exchanges and the possibilities of degradation.

12. Increased identification among inmates results from their experiencing conflict with the staff.

THE FINDINGS

The Characteristics and Consequences of Protest

Protest was found to be strongly related to rule violations and to specific behabior which has a clear-cut dominance meaning. Since recorded rule violations are highly selective, they tell us something about the response of the staff as well as about the behavior of the inmate. It is likely that the protesting inmate behaves in a way which is not merely non-conforming, but rather is an attack on the prison official's authority. Thus it eventually provokes the official into a hostile response. Protest was not found to be strongly related to specific behavior that has lacked a clear-cut dominance meaning. Avoiding riots may be high on the protestor's, as well as on the accommodator's, list of "do's." The protestor seems oriented toward relating to the officer in a way that expresses defiance of prison personnel but does not bring on a serious counterattack. Thus he maintains a favorable exchange. However, the data on rule violations suggest that his behavior does provoke some of the prison personnel. The data above offer support for the propositions suggesting that the protestor is dominance oriented and that he tends to provoke others into a dominance-oriented relationship toward himself. The same implications follow from the finding that protest relates strongly to attitudes toward the authority-oriented custody group and less strongly to attitudes toward the permissive treatment group.

Perception of Staff

Protest is highly correlated with the perception that the staff has little sympathy for inmates. Two of our hypotheses explain protest by reference to the status-threatening qualities of an unfavorable exchange. These hypotheses are consistent with data showing that inmates who hold an unfavorable view of staff attitudes are also high in protest.

Perception of Inmates

The data on perception of inmates affirms that protesting, as contrasted to accommodating, inmates feel themselves to be more at ease with other inmates, more interested by them, more similar to them; in short, protestors experience a greater sense of equality with other inmates. These findings offer some confirmation of the hypothesis that conflict leads to identification. However, protestors do not like inmates any more than do accommodators and even have a tendency to be more negative than accommodators in their rating of the inmates' importance. Feelings of similarity may not lead to liking in a situation in which the group has an overwhelming negative evaluation by the outside world.

Perception of Self

If an inmate views himself as having the characteristic attitudes of a square John, if he identifies with pro-social values, he is likely to be low in protest and to decrease in protest during his stay in the prison. This finding is consistent with the view that such an individual will experience relatively fewer unfavorable exchanges because he will not perceive the staff demands as emanating from staff whims. However, our data are consistent with earlier studies showing that the square John is likely to change his self view. As he acquires time in the institution, it is likely that his social type will change.

Negotiated Reward

The data from the instrumentalism scale suggest that con politicians and outlaws are oriented toward gaining the maximum amount of privilege in their relationships with the staff. The outlaw perceives himself as willing to negotiate under any conditions, but the con politician is likely to insist on a favorable view of himself by the staff as a precondition for negotiation. His self-conception would seem to require sympathy as a condition for his success in the negotiation process. The hypothesis stating that concern with negotiated reward leads to an unfavorable view of staff attitudes and, in turn, results in threat received little support from the instrumentalism scale. Sympathy was not related to scores on the instrumentalism scale. The data on protest and instrumentalism indicate that high protest is associated with high instrumentalism, but also with low instrumentalism. This suggests a reformulation of the negotiated reward hypothesis to read: A moderate degree of concern with negotiated reward leads an individual to curb his hostile acts toward the staff, but a focal concern with negotiated reward has the anticipated effect of increasing protest. There is an obvious implication here for penal administrators who hold that "every privilege must be earned."

Social Structure

Informal social relations. The hypothesis that an anti-staff group will cause an increase in its members' protest level gets a weak substantiation. Only those with friends who are perceived as outlaws show a strong upward change in protest. Those with square John friends show a downward trend; however, such inmates may be isolated from the society of prisoners.

When friends are classified as to their dominance orientation on the basis of responses to the instrumentalism scale, a more striking finding emerges. Those with dominance-oriented friends tend to be high on protest and to move upward. Those with non-dominance-oriented friends are likely to be low and to move downward on protest. The orientation of self has considerably less effect.

Membership in a dominance-oriented friendship group results in an increase in protest, regardless of the orientation of the inmate himself. Apparently the dominance-oriented group does not change the inmate's level of protest by articulating a negative view of staff attitudes. Sympathy scores are unrelated to position in the self-friends matrix. Although non-dominance friends include right guys and hence tend to provide an "anti-staff culture," their members do not show high protest or an increase in protest. The analysis of the self-friends matrix provides support for the "audience effect" hypothesis as well as for the relation of negotiated reward (instrumentalism) to dominance orientation.

Social position. Low social status increases protest and decreases sympathy; high status does not have the opposite effect. Indeed, an increase in status brings with it an increase in protest and a decrease in sympathy. This was interpreted as evidence that status shifts in any direction increase concern with dominance. Surprisingly, social status is not related to static protest, suggesting that the effect of social position upon protest may be transitory. In general, the analysis of change led to stronger findings than did the analysis of static variables.

Time served. The greater the time served, the less favorable the perception of staff attitudes toward inmates and the higher the level of protest. However, a reversal of this trend was noted just prior to release on parole. But time served has different effects on different inmates. Only those who interpret behavior in a highly personalistic fashion tend to increase in protest and decrease in sympathy. This finding supports the hypothesis that those who perceive acts as having a situational origin are less likely to interpret negative *acts* directed toward themselves as signs of negative *attitudes* toward themselves. Doubtless, negative acts are omnipresent in prison life, but they do not seem to lead to protest among the impersonalistic inmates.

Protest versus Sympathy

The hypothesis that persons will find unfavorable exchanges threatening to their self-esteem received its strongest support from the findings on protest-sympathy pairs and attitude change. Although the findings were statistically weak, the logical fit of the hypothesis to the data was excellent. Various relationships between protest level and sympathy level were examined. It was hypothesized, for example, that high protest and a view of the staff as highly sympathetic is not a stressful state. On the other hand, an inmate having a low-protest and low-sympathy score was predicted to be in a stressful state in which upward change would occur in both variables. These predictions were confirmed by the data.

The predictions that flow from the balance hypotheses of Gouldner and Homans did not get support from these data. By combining the status-threat hypothesis with some likely inferences about objective staff responses, an ever more complete empirical fit was obtained. In its final form the theory predicts that protest and sympathy may increase, but will not decrease, simultaneously.

In general, the variables examined herein have demonstrated more power in predicting unfavorable changes in attitude than they have in predicting favorable changes in attitude. Only in the case of the inmate who identifies himself with the pro-social world, i.e., the square John, do we find strongly favorable changes in attitude. The status-threat hypothesis, which identifies certain restrictions on favorable attitude change, may help to explain the trend of our findings. Further research, oriented toward the study of individuals who experience striking changes in their social-psychological world, would provide a crucial test of this notion.

BIBLIOGRAPHY

Adorno, T.W., et al. *The Authoritarian Personality.* New York: Harper and Brothers, 1950.

Baveles, Alex. "Research on Communication," in Seminar on Social Science for Industry (eds.). *Proceedings,* No. 3. Menlo Park, California, 1955.

Bettleheim, Bruno. "Individual and Mass Behavior in Crisis Situations," *Journal of Abnormal and Social Psychology,* XXXVIII (October, 1943).

Blalock, Hubert M. *Social Statistics.* New York: McGraw-Hill Book Co., 1960.

Boulding, Kenneth E. *Conflict and Defense.* New York: Harper and Bros., 1962.

Brehm, Jack W., and Arthur R. Cohen. *Explorations in Cognitive Dissonance.* New York: John Wiley and Sons, Inc., 1962.

Cantril, Hadley. *The Politics of Despair.* New York: Basic Books, 1958.

Caplow, Theodore. *The Sociology of Work.* Minneapolis: University of Minnesota Press, 1954.

Cartwright, Dorwin (ed.). *Studies in Social Power.* Ann Arbor: Research Center for Group Dynamics, University of Michigan, 1959.

Cartwright, Dorwin, and Alvin Zander. *Group Dynamics.* Evanston: Row, Peterson and Co., 1956.

Clemmer, Donald. *The Prison Community.* New York: Rinehart and Co., 1958.

Cloward, Richard A. "Illegitimate Means, Anomie, and Deviant Behavior," *American Sociological Review,* XXIV (April, 1959), 164-176.

Cloward, Richard A., and Lloyd E. Ohlin. *Delinquency and Opportunity.* Glencoe: The Free Press, 1960.

Cohen, Albert K. *Delinquent Boys.* Glencoe: The Free Press, 1955.

Coleman, James S. *Community Conflict.* Glencoe: The Free Press, 1957.

Coser, Lewis A. "The Termination of Conflict," *The Journal of Conflict Resolution*, V: 4 (December, 1961), 347-353.

_____. *The Functions of Social Conflict*. Glencoe: The Free Press, 1956.

Cressey, Donald R. (ed.). *The Prison*. New York: Holt, Rinehart, and Winston, 1961.

Cressey, Donald R., and John Irwin. "Thieves, Convicts, and the Inmate Culture," *Social Problems*, X (Fall, 1962), 142-145.

Dahrendorf, Ralf. *Class and Class Conflict in an Industrial Society*. Stanford: Stanford University Press, 1959.

Dubin, Robert. *Human Relations in Administration*. New York: Prentice-Hall, 1951.

Edwards, Allen L. *Techniques of Attitude Scale Construction*. New York: Appleton-Century-Crofts, Inc., 1957.

Festinger, Leon. "Cognitive Consequences of Forced Compliance," *Journal of Abnormal and Social Psychology*, LVIII (1959), 203-210.

_____. *A Theory of Cognitive Dissonance*. Evanston: Row, Peterson and Co., 1957.

Carabedian, Peter G. "Social Roles and the Process of Socialization in a Prison Community," *Social Problems*, II (Fall, 1963), 139-152.

_____. "Western Penitentiary: A Study in Social Organization," Unpublished Ph.D. dissertation, University of Washington, Seattle, 1959.

Gittler, Joseph B. *Review of Sociology: Analysis of a Decade*. New York: John Wiley and Sons, Inc., 1957.

Goffman, Erving. *Asylums*. New York: Anchor Books, 1961.

_____. *The Presentation of Self in Everyday Life*. New York: Anchor Books, 1959.

_____. *Encounters*. Indianapolis: Bobbs-Merrill Co., 1961.

Gouldner, Alvin. *Patterns of Industrial Bureaucracy*. Glencoe: The Free Press, 1954.

Grosser, George A. H. (ed.). *Theoretical Studies in the Social Organization of the Prison*. New York: Social Science Research Council, 1960. Pamphlet No.

Gulliksen, Harold. *Theory of Mental Tests*. New York: John Wiley and So

Heider, Fritz. *The Psychology of Interpersonal Relations.* New York: John Wiley and Sons, 1958.

Henderson, A. M., and Talcott Parsons (eds.). *Max Weber: The Theory of Social and Economic Organization.* New York: Oxford University Press, 1947.

Himelson, Alfred, and Paul Takagi. *Research Report No. 7.* Research Division, Department of Corrections, Youth and Adult Corrections Agency, State of California.

Homans, George C. *The Human Group.* New York: Harcourt, Brace and Co., 1950.

_____. *Social Behavior: Its Elementary Forms.* New York: Harcourt, Brace and Co., 1961.

Hoyt, Cyril. "Test Reliability Obtained by Analysis of Variance," *Psychometrike,* VI, 153-160.

Kardiner, Abraham, and Lionel Ovesey. *The Mark of Oppression.* New York: W.W. Norton and Co., 1951.

Kinch, John W. "Certain Social Psychological Aspects of Types of Juvenile Delinquents." Unpublished Ph.D. dissertation, University of Washington, Seattle, 1959.

Kogon, Eugene. *The Theory and Practice of Hell.* New York: Berkeley, 1960.

Lipset, Seymour M. *Political Man.* New York: Doubleday, 1959.

Marks, Eli S., Charles E. Fritz, et al. "Human Reactions in Disaster Situations." Unpublished report, National Opinion Research Center, University of Chicago, June, 1954, Vol. I.

Mayo, Elton. *The Social Problems of an Industrial Civilization.* Boston: Harvard University, 1945.

McCorkle, Lloyd W., Albert Elias, and T. Lovell Bixby. *The Highfields Story.* New York: Henry Holt and Co., 1958.

McNemar, Quinn *Psychological Statistics.* Third edition. New York: John Wiley , 1962.

Social Theory and Social Structure. Revised edition. Glencoe: s, 1957.

ructure and Anomie," *American Sociological Review,* III (Octo-
-682.

-138-

Merton, Robert K., Leonard Broom, and Leonard S. Cottrell (eds.). Sociology Today. New York: Basic Books, 1959.

Merton, Robert K., and Robert A. Nisbet (eds.). Contemporary Social Problems. New York: Harcourt, Brace and World, 1961.

Miller, Walter B. "Lower Class Culture as a Generating Milieu of Gang Delinquency," Journal of Social Issues, XIV: 3 (1958), 5-19.

Milosz, Czeslaw. The Captive Mind. New York: Alfred A. Knopf, 1953.

Morgenthau, Hans J. Politics among Nations. New York: Alfred A. Knopf, 1948.

Newcomb, Theodore M. The Acquaintance Process. New York: Rinehart and Winston, 1961.

Osgood, Charles E., and Percy H. Tannenbaum. "The Principle of Congruity in the Prediction of Attitude Change," Psychological Review (January, 1955), 349-353.

Osgood, Charles E., George J. Suci, and Percy Tannenbaum. The Measurement of Meaning. Urbana: University of Illinois Press, 1957.

Park, Robert E. "Human Ecology," American Journal of Sociology, XLII (July, 1936), 1-15.

Redl, Fritz, and David Wineman. Children Who Hate. New York: The Free Press, 1951.

Roethlisberger, F.J., and William J. Dickson. Management and the Worker. Cambridge: Harvard University Press, 1939.

Rothbart, George S. "Ideology and Strategy: A Study of Attitudes toward the Organizational Process." Unpublished Master's thesis, University of Washington, Seattle, 1962.

Sayles, Leonard. Behavior of Industrial Work Groups. New York: John Wiley and Sons, 1958.

Schelling, Thomas C. The Strategy of Conflict. Cambridge: Harvard University Press, 1960.

Schrag, Clarence C. "Social Types in a Prison Community." Unpublished Master's thesis, University of Washington, Seattle, 1944.

Schumpeter, J.A. Capitalism, Socialism, and Democracy. New York: Harper and Brothers, 1950.

Scudder, Kenyon J. Prisoners are People. New York: Doubleday, 1952.

Sherif, Muzafer, et al. *Intergroup Conflict and Cooperation: The Robber's Cave Experiment.* Norman: Institute of Group Relations, University of Oklahoma, 1961.

Simmel, George. *Conflict and the Web of Group Affiliations.* Glencoe: The Free Press, 1955.

State of Washington, Department of Institutions. *Research Review*, No. VIII, 1962.

Stouffer, Samuel A., et al. *The American Soldier,* Vol. I. Princeton: Princeton University Press, 1949.

Sutherland, Edwin H. *Principles of Criminology.* Fourth edition. Philadelphia: J.B. Lippincott Co., 1947.

Sykes, Gresham M. *The Society of Captives.* Princeton: Princeton University Press, 1958.

_____. "The Corruption of Authority and Rehabilitation," *Social Forces,* XXXIV (March, 1956), 257-262.

Sykes, Gresham M., and David Matza. "Techniques of Neutralization: A Theory of Delinquency," *American Sociological Review,* XXII (December, 1957), 664-670.

Thrasher, Frederic M. *The Gang.* Chicago: University of Chicago Press, 1927.

Vold, George. *Theoretical Criminology.* New York: Oxford University Press, 1958.

Weeks, Ashley. *Youthful Offenders at Highfields.* Ann Arbor: University of Michigan Press, 1958.

Wheeler, Stanton. "Socialization in Correctional Communities," *American Sociological Review,* XXVI (October, 1961), 299-712.

_____. "Social Organization in a Correctional Community." Unpublished Ph.D. dissertation, University of Washington, Seattle, 1958.

Witmer, Helen Leland, and Ruth Kotinsky (eds.). *New Perspectives for Research on Juvenile Delinquency.* Washington, D.C.: United States Department of Health, ___lfare, Children's Bureau Publication No. 356, 1956.

APPENDIX A

LETTER OF SOLICITATION TO INMATES

TO:_____NUMBER_____CELL_____

FROM: MR._____, SOCIOLOGIST

FORD FOUNDATION CORRECTIONAL

EVALUATION STUDY

You may have heard about the Ford Foundation research program here at the Reformatory. The Ford Foundation is a private organization providing money to support research on prison life. A number of researchers from the University of Washington are beginning a new part of the program shortly. They would like you to participate in this part of the program. It is up to you to decide whether to take part or not.

All people who take part will be asked to fill out a series of questionnaires, and some will be asked to be in some discussion groups. I have a feeling that this program will prove to be important and that you will find it interesting, too. In addition, you will be paid (from one dollar to four dollars) for taking part, depending on the number of things you are asked to take part in.

Since different parts of the questionnaire will be filled out at different times, they will ask you to give your number so that your different questionnaires can be put together. However, the researchers guarantee that your questionnaires will be <u>absolutely confidential.</u> No member of the staff, including myself, will <u>ever</u> be able to look at your questionnaire.

If you want to volunteer, please fill out the form below, and place it in the box labeled <u>RESEARCH</u> in the sally port no later than 4 P.M., Thursday, June 14, 1962. Thank you!

NOTE: If you volunteer, you will be notified within a few days as to when the project will begin.

If you are currently on A side, you are still able to participate in this program. A special time will be arranged for your participation.

APPENDIX B

THE QUESTIONNAIRE INSTRUMENTS

INSTRUMENTS USING LIKERT-TYPE FORMAT

Five different sets of items were given in one section of the questionnaire, using a single format. They were the:

1. Protest scale
2. Sympathy scale
3. Reward Scale
4. Items measuring overt conflict behavior
5. Self-type scale

The format was as follows:

Read each of the statements below and then answer them as follows:

A	a	n	d	D
strongly agree	mildly agree	neither agree nor disagree	mildly disagree	strongly disagree

Indicate your opinion by drawing a circle around the (A) if you strongly agree, around the (a) if you mildly agree, around the (d) if you mildly disagree, around the (D) if you strongly disagree. If you neither agree nor disagree, draw a circle around the (n). There are no right or wrong answers, so answer the statements according to your own opinions. It is very important that all questions be answered. Many statements will seem alike, but all are necessary to show slight differences of opinion. You will see that we use the words, "treatment staff." By "treatment staff" we mean classification counselors, teachers, psychologists, sociologists, etc.

(Circle one letter for each statement)

	Strongly	Mildly	Neither	Mildly	Strongly
1. Item 1	A	a	n	d	D
2. Item 2	A	a	n	d	D
etc.					

The Protest Scale

1. An inmate should usually try to "go along" with what the staff wants . . . . . (R)

2. When a riot starts in a prison, it is usually because the inmates have been pushed too far . . . .

3. Inmates ought to try soft-pedaling some of their complaints and try saying a few nice things to the staff once in a while . . . . (R)

4. Riots are the worst things that can happen in a prison . . . . (R)

5. The trouble with most inmates is that they have a bad attitude against the staff . . . . (R)

6. The inmates in this place don't stick up for their rights . . . .

7. Inmates should try the soft approach for a change in making their wishes known to the prison staff . . . . (R)

8. I feel pretty strong about some of the complaints that we inmates have . . . .

9. When a big inmate blow-up starts in a prison, it is usually justified . . . . .

10. In prison, it is sometimes a good idea to "give in" a little to avoid trouble and arguments with the staff . . . . (R)

    (In Questionnaire One, the above item read: "In prison, it is sometimes necessary to ignore what you think is right and 'give in' a little to avoid trouble and arguments with the staff.")

11. I don't mind hurrying along when I'm doing something if it's necessary in order to make the institutional time schedule run O.K. . . . . (R)

12. Needs of the inmates are often ignored because the staff can buy off a few inmate leaders and "to hell with the rest" . . . .

13. It's not a bad thing if the staff gets some trouble from the inmates every once in a while . . . .

14. One thing I don't like to do is address all the officers as "Mister" . . . . . .

15. There is no good reason to be different when visitors are around, even if the staff wants us to . . . .

Items not marked (R) received a score of 0 if for a "strongly disagree" endorsement, 1 for "mildly disagree," 2 for "neither," 3 for "mildly agree," and 4 for "strongly agree."

Items marked (R) were scored in the reverse direction. They received a score of 4 for a "strongly disagree" endorsement, 3 for "mildly disagree," 2 for "neither," 1 for "mildly agree," and 0 for "strongly agree."

Only items 2, 4, 6, 10, 12, and 13 were used in the second questionnaire.

The Sympathy Scale

1. The people on the staff here seem to feel that an inmate can never be trusted. (R)

2. Many of the staff members here have sympathy for the inmates' point of view.

3. In this reformatory, the only persons you can really talk your personal problems over with are friends among your fellow inmates ....(R)

4. The people on the staff here feel that you are more than just a case history...

5. Most of the treatment staff here believe "once a con, always a con."..........(R)

6. Rules here at the reformatory have been made up with consideration for the inmates' wishes...

7. Staff members are not interested in you, but only in your record.............(R)

8. Most of the correctional officers here believe "once a con, always a con."....(R)

The scoring technique was the same as for the protest scale.

Only items 2, 3, 5, 6, and 8 were used in the second questionnaire.

The Reward Scale

1. If the inmates do just what the staff wants them to do, they get pretty good privileges around here...

2. As far as I can tell, they have a pretty good rehabilitation program around this institution...

3. In here an inmate is made to feel like a caged animal.......................

4. In this institution, the correctional officers will give you a write-up whenever they feel like it, whether there is a good reason or not......................

The scoring technique was the same as for the protest scale.

Only items 1 and 2 were used in the second questionnaire.

Items measuring Overt Conflict Behavior

1. I often throw food on the mess hall floor.

2. One thing I won't do is address all the officers as "Mister."

The above items were not scored so as to form a scale.

The Self-Type Scale

The following chart shows the items and the direction in which they were scored for each of the Schrag social types. An index was computed for each social type by adding up the scores received on that type, for each item.

	Square John	Con politician	Outlaw	Right Guy	Double weight for
1. It makes me sore to have people tell me what to do	−	−	+	−	Outlaw
2. I am not trusted by other inmates	+	−	+	−	
3. In prison it is sometimes a good idea to "give in" a little to avoid trouble and arguments with the staff	+	+	−	−	
4. I have a lot of friends on the outside	+	+	−	−	
5. The only criminals I really know are the ones here inside the reformatory	+	−	−	−	Square John
6. If other inmates are counting on me, I'll do my best for the inmates in this place	−	−	−	+	Right guy
7. I am clever in getting what I want from reformatory officials	−	+	−	−	Con politician
8. I really know what is going on here at the reformatory	−	+	−	+	

Types marked + (plus) on an item received a score of 4 for "strongly agree," 3 for "mildly agree," 2 for "neither," 1 for "mildly disagree," and 0 for "strongly disagree." Types marked - (minus) on an item were scored in the reverse direction by giving them a score of 4 for "strongly disagree," 3 for "mildly disagree," etc. The types that were marked double weight on an item received 8 instead of 4, 6 instead of 3, etc.

The inmate was put into the type category corresponding to his largest score. Some inmates had to be put into a "tied" category.

FRIENDS' TYPE SCALE

On the following pages is a section of the friendship instrument. The inmates were asked to write the names of ten friends in the spaces provided at the top of the sheet. They were told, "We are not trying to get you to give us information about specific people, but we want you to do a job for us with the ten names. When you are through, we want you to tear off the list of names and throw it away. Please give us the names of the first ten friends you can think of, not just your best friends." We used a colored cover sheet so as to reduce the inmates' tendency to open the page and look at the questions. The green sheet was so visible that few inmates attempted to satisfy their curiosity. When they were instructed to open the sheet, they found a page with a series of statements, with Yes-No responses lined up below the first name. The inmates were told to circle "Yes" if the statement described the person correction, and to circle "no" if it did not. The second page repeated the same questions for the second person, and so on, through eight more pages for eight more names. The last page included a single item about the whole group of friends.

Each friend was put in a type category by determining whether he fit any of the following patterns:

	Square John	Outlaw	Con politician	Right guy
1. He is trusted by other inmates	+/−	+/−	+	+
2. He is a leader among the inmates	−	−	+/−	+/−
3. He really knows what's going on around here	−	−	+	+
4. He is clever in getting what he wants from reformatory officials	−	−	+	−
5. It makes him sore to have people tell him what to do	−	+	−	+/−

A residual category included all other patterns. After scoring each friend, the inmate was classified according to the type prevailing among his friends, on the basis of numerical majority. If there was a tie between any of the four type categories, the inmate was scored as "tied." If any of the types were tied with the residual category, the type rather than the residual category was used. If the residual category was larger than any of the types, the residual category, not the tied category was used. The second item on the sheet describing the friends was not utilized, even though it was appropriate to the square John type. The Yes-No response format, it turned out, produced some confusion in responding to that item.

1.	2.	3.	4.	5.	6.	7.	8.	9.	10.

Yes No   He is a leader among the inmates.

Yes No   He is not really a criminal.

Yes No   It makes him sore to have people tell him what to do.

Yes No   He is trusted by other inmates.

Yes No   He is clever in getting what he wants from reformatory officials.

Yes No   He is a good friend of mine.

Yes No   He really knows what's going on around here.

Yes No   I often eat lunch at the same table with him.

1.	2.	3.	4.	5.	6.	7.	8.	9.	10.

Yes No   He is a leader among the inmates

Yes No   He is not really a criminal.

Yes No   It makes him sore to have people tell him what to do.

Yes No   He is trusted by other inmates.

Yes No   He is clever in getting what he wants from reformatory officials.

Yes No   He is a good friend of mine.

Yes No   He really knows what's going on around here.

Yes No   I often eat lunch at the same table with him.

1.	2.	3.	4.	5.	6.	7.	8.	9.	10.

Of the people you mentioned, about how many would you say know one another?

_____ nearly all know one another
_____ about 3/4 "   "   "
_____ about 1/2 "   "   "
_____ about 1/4 "   "   "
_____ almost none know one another

INSTRUMENTALISM SCALE

The instrumentalism scale is reproduced below. The numbers in parentheses are the scores appropriate to each possible item endorsement. A 4 indicates that the response category represents the maximum degree of instrumentalism. The same scale was used on all three questionnaires.

Below you are asked to indicate whether you agree or disagree with some things that inmates did in other institutions. Read each story and then tell us how you feel about the inmates' actions as follows:

strongly agree	mildly agree	neither agree nor disagree	mildly disagree	strongly disagree
A	a	n	d	D

Indicate your opinion by drawing a circle around the (A) if you strongly agree, around the (a) if you mildly agree, around the (d) if you mildly disagree, around the (D) if you strongly disagree. If you neither agree nor disagree, draw a circle around the (n) There are no right or wrong answers, so answer according to your own opinion. <u>Circle only one letter for each story.</u>

STORIES

1. Inmates in one reformatory were getting pretty fed up with the movies that they were seeing. Most of the moview were very old and they saw some of them several times. The inmates complained to the staff and they were told "Quit your complaining or we will cut out the movies altogether." Some of the inmates started talking about pulling a hunger strike. Actually, the inmates heard that the warden was worrying about the people in the state capitol and there was a pretty good

chance that he might give in. The inmates decided that they had better play it cool and put up with the movies.

How do you personally feel about the inmates' actions?

strongly agree	mildly agree	neither agree nor disagree	mildly disagree	strongly disagree
A	a	n	d	D
(0)	(1)	(2)	(3)	(4)

2. In a prison in the midwest, the food was pretty bad and the inmates were pretty unhappy about it. The warden told them to quit complaining. The inmates in one cell block began talking about starting some big trouble. If they did, they probably would get better food since the warden wanted to keep the inmates quiet. The inmates started trouble by plugging up the toilets and flooding out the cell block.

How do you personally feel about the inmates' actions?

strongly agree	mildly agree	neither agree nor disagree	mildly disagree	strongly disagree
A	a	n	d	D
(4)	(3)	(2)	(1)	(0)

3. At a reformatory they were having official visitors from the state capitol. The food had not been too good lately, but on this day they were getting fried chicken. The staff quietly passed the word around that they wanted everyone to look good for the visitors. If they didn't, the warden probably would get irritated and cut privileges. A bunch of inmates started to push and shove in the line while the visitors were watching.

How do you personally feel about the inmates' actions?

strongly agree	mildly agree	neither agree nor disagree	mildly disagree	strongly disagree
A	a	n	d	D
(0)	(1)	(2)	(3)	(4)

4. In one prison the warden was very tough about getting the men into their houses on time at lock-up. In one cell block the inmates have had a lot of write-ups and the whole block lost privileges for getting into their houses late. They talked it over with one another and decided they had better start getting into their houses on time.

How do you personally feel about the inmates' actions?

strongly agree	mildly agree	neither agree nor disagree	mildly disagree	strongly disagree
A	a	n	d	D
(4)	(3)	(2)	(1)	(0)

THE PERSONALISM SCALE

The personalism scale is reproduced below. (1) indicates the responses that were scored as personal; (0) indicates an impersonal response. Items 1-8 were used in the first two questionnaires; all the items were used in the third questionnaire.

On the following pages you will find some little stories about people in prisons and other places. First of all, read the stories carefully. Below the stories are some reasons that people have suggested as to why the persons in the stories did the things they did. For each story we have given two of the reasons. We want you to tell us which one of the two is the most likely reason, in your opinion. Of course, there may be other reasons besides the ones we have listed. But you are to guess which of the two that are listed you think might come closest to the truth.

1. Canwell, an inmate, has a poor record in the reformatory. He has gotten himself a lot of write-ups for rule infractions and has a poor work record. However, he recently has been trying hard and has shown some improvement. Canwell's case worker recommends that Canwell should not be given early parole.

    What is the best guess you can make as to why the case worker did this?

    (0) Canwell is likely to violate parole; and as a result, the case worker fears that he will be criticized by his boss.

    (1) The case worker doesn't like Canwell. If he did, he would probably give Canwell the benefit of the doubt and recommend early parole.

2. Mrs. Lander is driving down the street in her automobile. At a stop sign, another driver does not see Mrs. Lander's hand signal, failes to stop in time, and hits Mrs. Lander's car. The result is a little damage to the rear end of Mrs. Lander's car. Mrs. Lander gets very upset and bawls out the other driver.

    What is your best guess as to why Mrs. Lander got so upset?

    (0) She is afraid that when her husband finds out that she has been in an accident, he will get angry at her.

    (1) She is probably the kind of person who loses her temper very easily.

3. Jones does very well on his job and gets himself a very fat raise in salary. He buys himself a set of golf clubs and begins spending his spare time at a local golf club. A few months later he buys himself a brand new sport car.

   What is your best guess as to why Jones bought the sport car?

   __(1)__ He has always wanted one and now he can afford one.

   __(0)__ His new friends at the golf club probably expect him to live in a pretty good style.

4. Inmate Randall works in the furniture factory in a state reformatory in the Midwest. He has a pretty good job that is near the top of the pay scale. He gets in an argument with the supervisor, curses him out, and loses his job.

   What is your best guess as to why Randall did all these things?

   __(1)__ He probably doesn't know how to get along with people. If he did, this wouldn't have happened to him.

   __(0)__ The other men in the work crew have a lot of gripes about their jobs, Randall has just been "blowing off steam" for the whole work crew.

(In Questionnaire One, the last alternative read, "The Supervisor has been pushing him around and working him very hard. Any man would have gotten mad.")

5. Green, an officer, has a strong attitude against inmate Thomas. He has heard a lot of bad reports on Thomas that were started by another officer. Actually, these reports were all wrong.

   What is your best guess as to why Green has this attitude?

   __(0)__ He spends most of his time talking to other officers and would naturally tend to believe what he heard.

   __(1)__ He probably isn't interested in Thomas. If we were, he would check out the reports and find out that they were untrue.

6. Inmate Dynes is about to be shifted to the honor farm. One day the captain asks the name of the inmate who started a fight in the yard a few days earlier. Dynes refuses to tell the captain and is kept inside the walls.

   What is your best guess as to why Dynes refused?

   __(0)__ Dynes doesn't want to get another inmate in trouble.

   __(1)__ Dynes is probably a buddy of the inmate who started the fight.

7. Inmate Jones is feeling pretty sick to his stomach. He talks to one of the officers about his trouble and the officer calls the doctor about it and gives Jones a sick-call slip.

   What is your best guess as to why the officer did this?

   (0) It is his job to see that the inmates get to the doctor when they need one.

   (1) He probably is the kind of officer who is friendly toward inmates.

8. Johnson, an officer, sees an inmate taking a lot of time walking to his cell at final lock-up time. He doesn't do anything about it and just lets him loaf along.

   What is your best guess as to why Johnson did this?

   (1) He and the inmate are pretty friendly.

   (0) Johnson has recently been going to lectures on "The Principles of Good Rehabilitation," and has heard that it is not a good idea to always be bawling out the inmates.

9. Inmate Brown was dropped out of vocational school for showing up late a few times and being "laid-in" too many times for one reason or another.

   What is your best guess as to why the vocational teacher dropped inmate Brown?

   (0) The teacher is following the rules. He is afraid that if he didn't drop Brown a lot of other inmates would follow Brown's example.

   (1) He probably has it "in" for Brown. He probably makes exceptions to the rules for the guys he likes.

10. Inmate Smith runs across some pruno hidden by inmate Vincent. He'd like to take a drink of it since he hasn't tasted the stuff in quite a while. Vincent is a leader among the inmates. Smith decides to leave Vincent's pruno alone.

    What is your best guess as to why Smith did this?

    (1) He is afraid of what might happen to him if Vincent found out that he drank the pruno.

    (0) He doesn't want to steal from another inmate, regardless of who the inmate happens to be.

THE SEMANTIC DIFFERENTIALS

The following three objects were used:

1. Inmates.

2. Custody staff (correctional officers, sergeants, lieutenants, captains of custody).

3. Treatment staff (classification counselors, teachers, psychologists, sociologists, etc.).

The scalettes and response categories are reproduced below:

hard	___:___:___:___:___:___	soft
selfish	___:___:___:___:___:___	unselfish
fair	___:___:___:___:___:___	unfair
tense	___:___:___:___:___:___	relaxed
stable	___:___:___:___:___:___	unstable
dull	___:___:___:___:___:___	interesting
good	___:___:___:___:___:___	bad
similar to me	___:___:___:___:___:___	different from me
weak	___:___:___:___:___:___	strong
excited	___:___:___:___:___:___	calm
free to do things	___:___:___:___:___:___	forced to do things
important	___:___:___:___:___:___	unimportant
careful	___:___:___:___:___:___	careless
masculine	___:___:___:___:___:___	feminine
foolish	___:___:___:___:___:___	wise
sympathetic	___:___:___:___:___:___	unsympathetic
bossy	___:___:___:___:___:___	not bossy
I like	___:___:___:___:___:___	I dislike

The following instructions were used. They were supplemented by illustrations, using a blackboard.

INSTRUCTIONS

At the top of each of the following pages you will find a word like "money" or "inmate." Below the word you will find some "scales" for describing how you feel about the thing the word stands for.

The following example will illustrate how you are to respond:

SCHOOL

important __X__:_____:_____:_____:_____:_____:_____ unimportant

hard _____:_____:__X__:_____:_____:_____:_____ soft

In this illustration the word SCHOOL is to be described according to how you feel about it. Suppose you think that school is very important. Then you would put an X in the space at the end nearest "important" that means "very important," as shown above. Of course, if you thought that school was unimportant, you would put your X somewhere on the other end of the scale to tell how unimportant you thought it was. Then move on down to the next "scale." Suppose you think that school is slightly hard. Then you would put an X in the space that indicates "slightly hard," as shown above. Then you would move on down to the next "scale" and so on until you come to the bottom of the page.

THE SOCIAL BACKGROUND ITEMS

Some Information about Your Background

1. From the list below, please check the offense for which you are now serving your sentence.

   _____ Assault
   _____ Auto theft
   _____ Burglary or grand larceny
   _____ Carnal knowledge
   _____ Forgery or grand larceny by check
   _____ Homicide
   _____ Indecent liberties
   _____ Probation violation
   _____ Parole violation
   _____ Robbery
   _____ Rape
   _____ Other Offense (specify)
   _____

2. If you checked "Parole violation" or "Probation violation" to the above question, please specify the offense for which you were committed before you were paroled or placed on probation.

   _____

3. Were you ever arrested <u>before</u> the arrest for the offense for which you are now serving your sentence?

   _____ Yes, 5 or more times
   _____ Yes, 3 or 4 times
   _____ Yes, 1 or 2 times
   _____ No

4. How old were you when you were arrested for the first time?

   _____ Under 14
   _____ 14 to 17
   _____ 18 to 20
   _____ 21 to 23
   _____ over 23

5. Prior to the offense for which you are now serving your sentence, were you ever committed to a reformatory or penitentiary?

   _____ Yes, twice or more
   _____ Yes, once
   _____ No

6. Were you ever committed to a juvenile training school or any type of juvenile correctional institution?

   _____ Yes
   _____ No

7. How old were you on your last birthday?

   _____

8. What is your educational background?

   _____ No school
   _____ Some grammar school
   _____ Completed grammar school (8th grade)
   _____ Some high school
   _____ Completed high school
   _____ Some college

About your sentence:

1. On what date were you admitted to Monroe for your present commitment?

   Month_____ Day_____ Year_____

2. What is your present release date?

   Month_____ Day_____ Year_____

3. Have you been before the Parole Board in the last two months?

   _____ Yes
   _____ No

   If Yes, did you get a cut in your sentence?

   _____ Yes (Specify how much)_____
   _____ No

THE "WHEELER" CONFORMITY ITEMS

The following two items are taken from a scale developed by Stanton Wheeler (and reported in his "Social Organization in a Correctional Community," unpublished Ph.D. dissertation, University of Washington, Seattle, 1958).

INSTRUCTIONS

Described on the following pages are actions inmates have taken in certain situations in correctional institutions. The statements do not refer to any particular inmate, or to any particular correctional institution. The institution might be a penitentiary, a reformatory, an honor camp, or a prison farm. For each statement, we would like to know first, how you personally feel about the action taken by the inmate. Then we would like to know how most reformatory inmates probably feel about the action. Finally, we would like to know how most staff members probably feel about the action.

Please read each description carefully. Then mark an X beside the statement that comes closest to your feeling. Then mark another X beside the statement that comes closest to your guess as to how most reformatory inmates would feel. Finally, mark another X beside the statement that comes closest to your guess as to how most staff members would feel.

Inmate Dooley gets cut in a knife fight with another inmate. Dooley is called before a disciplinary committee. The committee asks him to tell them who he was fighting with. He refuses to name the other inmate.

How do you personally feel about Dooley's refusal to name the other inmate? (Check one)

_____ Strongly approve of Dooley's action
_____ Approve of Dooley's action
_____ Disapprove of Dooley's action
_____ Strongly disapprove of Dooley's action

How many reformatory inmates do you think would <u>approve</u> of Dooley's action? (Check one)

_____ Almost all of them would approve
_____ About three-fourths of them would approve
_____ About half of them would approve
_____ About one-fourth of them would approve
_____ Almost none of them would approve

How many staff members do you think would <u>approve</u> of Dooley's action? (Check one)

_____ Almost all of them would approve
_____ About three-fourths of them would approve
_____ About half of them would approve
_____ About one-fourth of them would approve
_____ Almost none of them would approve

Inmates Smith and Long are very good friends. Smith has a five-dollar bill that was smuggled into the institution by a visitor. Smith tells Long he thinks the officers are suspicious and asks Long to hide the money for him for a few days. Long takes the money and carefully hides it.

How do you personally feel about Long's action? (Check one)

_____ Strongly approve of Long's action
_____ Approve of Long's action
_____ Disapprove of Long's action
_____ Strongly disapprove of Long's action

How many reformatory inmates do you think would <u>approve</u> of Long's action? (Check one)

_____ Almost all of them would approve
_____ About three-fourths of them would approve
_____ About half of them would approve
_____ About one-fourth of them would approve
_____ Almost none of them would approve

How many staff members do you think would <u>approve</u> of Long's action? (Check One)

    _____Almost all of them would approve
    _____About three-fourths of them would approve
    _____About half of them would approve
    _____About one-fourth of them would approve
    _____Almost none of them would approve

THE WORK CREW STATUS SCALE

The questionnaire pages that follow, entitled "About Work Assignments," provided the data for computing the desirability ranks of the various jobs available to inmates. Mean ratings of desirability were calculated by giving a "very desirable" response a score of three, "desirable" a score of two, "undesirable" a score of one, and "very undesirable" a score of zero. The work crews were then ranked, in order of the means. Moving down from the highest rank, the jobs were put into the category "high" until one-third of the prison population was included. The next one-third of the prison population was classified as "medium," and the lowest-ranking one-third was classified as "low." The following table lists the jobs in rank order, from low to high, with the number of men in each of the jobs, and the status category into which each job was placed. The number of inmates in the honor farm and forest camp is not shown, as these inmates were not considered in breaking up the prison population into thirds. In a very few cases, extrapolations about job desirability had to be made on the basis of ratings of similar jobs.

JOB TITLE	NUMBER IN CREW	WORK CREW STATUS
Yard maintenance	25	
Inmate kitchen	48	
Porter inside walls	57	Low
Mattress factory	22	
Laundry	25	
Clothing room	14	
Furniture factory	86	
Clerk in library	4	
Miscellaneous clerk	6	
Porter in administration building	4	
Maintenance and salvage	8	
Shoe shop	14	
Protective maintenance	8	Medium
Plumbing maintenance	6	
Dry cleaning shop	10	
Building trades	9	
Music and activities	5	
Mechanical maintenance	7	
continued		continued

-158-

JOB TITLE	NUMBER IN CREW	WORK CREW STATUS
Carpentry maintenance	13	
Garage	8	
Sheet metal shop	10	
Industry commissary	8	
Medical department	17	
Machine shop	10	
School all day	81	
Hobby shop	3	
Staff barber shop	2	
Commissary	2	High
Electrical maintenance	5	
Print shop	16	
Athletics	4	
Clerk, inmate store	2	
Inmate barber shop	14	
Radio and TV (not porter)	20	

ABOUT WORK ASSIGNMENTS

In places like Monroe, as well as on the outside, people often talk about whether a job is desirable or undesirable. We would like you to tell us your impressions of how desirable are certain jobs that are available to inmates at Monroe.

Below is a list of jobs and other assignments. Draw a circle around the letter that best expresses your feelings as to the desirability or undesirability of each job or other assignment on the list. If you feel you don't know enough about the job to be able to make a rating, circle (dk). <u>Please rate the job or assignment by comparison to other jobs or assignments at Monroe.</u>

(Use only one circle for each job or other assignment.)

	Very desirable	Desirable	Undesirable	Very undesirable	Don't know
1. The mattress factory (crew 8)	D	d	u	U	dk
2. Body and fender shop (crew 52)	D	d	u	U	dk
3. Clerk in the library (crew 48)	D	d	u	U	dk
4. Porter in the administration building (crew 3)	D	d	u	U	dk

		(Use only one circle for each job or other assignment.)				
		Very desirable	Desirable	Undesirable	Very undesirable	Don't know
5.	Porter inside the walls	D	d	u	U	dk
6.	Commissary crew (crew 11)	D	d	u	U	dk
7.	Garage (crew 42)	D	d	u	U	dk
8.	Inmate kitchen (crew 29)	D	d	u	U	dk
9.	Carpenter maintenance (crew 30)	D	d	u	U	dk
10.	Maintenance and salvage (crew 16)	D	d	u	U	dk
11.	Protective maintenance (crew 6)	D	d	u	U	dk
12.	Protective maintenance (crew 6)	D	d	u	U	dk
13.	Radio and TV shop (crew 37)	D	d	u	U	dk
14.	Dry cleaning shop (crew 36)	D	d	u	U	dk
15.	Electrical maintenance (crew 32)	D	d	u	U	dk
16.	Yard maintenance (crew 46)	D	d	u	U	dk
17.	Athletics (crew 45)	D	d	u	U	dk
18.	Sheet metal shop (crew 49)	D	d	u	U	dk
19.	Drafting shop (crew 50)	D	d	u	U	dk
20.	Industries commissary (crew 15, 11)	D	d	u	U	dk
21.	Inmate barber shop (crew 26)	D	d	u	U	dk
22.	Staff barber shop (crew 3)	D	d	u	U	dk
23.	Clothing room (crew 25)	D	d	u	U	dk
24.	School all day	D	d	u	U	dk
25.	Print shop (crew 43)	D	d	u	U	dk
26.	Carpenter maintenance (crew 51, 20)	D	d	u	U	dk
27.	Furniture factory (crew 41)	D	d	u	U	dk
28.	Clerk in inmate store (crew 22)	D	d	u	U	dk
29.	Building trades shop (crew 14)	D	d	u	U	dk
30.	Plumbing maintenance (crew 6, 31)	D	d	u	U	dk
31.	Medical department (crew 21)	D	d	u	U	dk
32.	Music and activities (crew 24)	D	d	u	U	dk
33.	Mechanical maintenance (crew 33)	D	d	u	U	dk
34.	Laundry (crew 35)	D	d	u	U	dk
35.	Machine shop (crew 39)	D	d	u	U	dk
36.	Clerk (rotunda, educ. floor, etc.)	D	d	u	U	dk
37.	Shoe shop (crew 40)	D	d	u	U	dk
38.	Honor farm	D	d	u	U	dk
39.	Forestry camp	D	d	u	U	dk

APPENDIX C

THE REGRESSED SCORES AND CUTTING POINTS

CALCULATION OF REGRESSED PROTEST SCORES

The following table shows the values of protest and sympathy change (from Time One to Time Three) predicted from scores at Time One. The predictions were made from a linear regression line calculated by the formula, $Y = a + bX$, where $b = \frac{\Sigma xy}{\Sigma y^2}$. Values are given only for scores that actually occurred. Regressed scores were calculated by subtracting predicted from actual score and adding 25 to the protest change score and 5 to the sympathy change score. For example, if a respondent received an initial protest score of 28, and a change score of 35, his regressed score would be $35 - 25 + 25 = 10$.

Protest score (Time One)	Predicted protest change score (rounded)	Sympathy score (Time One)	Predicted sympathy change score (rounded)
7	33	0	7
8	33	1	7
9	33	2	7
10	32	3	7
11	32	4	6
12	31	5	6
13	31	6	6
14	31	7	6
15	30	8	6
16	30	9	6
17	30	10	5
18	29	11	5
19	29	12	5
20	28	13	5
21	28	14	5
22	28	15	5
23	27	16	4
24	27	17	4
25	27	18	4
26	26	19	4
27	26	20	4
28	25	21	4
29	25	22	3
30	25	23	3
31	24	24	3
32	24	25	3

continued

Protest Score (Time One)	Predicted protest change score (rounded)	Sympathy score (Time One)	Predicted sympathy change score (rounded)
33	24	26	3
34	23	27	3
35	23	28	2
36	22	29	2
37	22	30	2
38	22	31	2
39	21		
40	21		
41	21		
42	20		
51	17		

CUTTING POINTS FOR PROTEST AND SYMPATHY SCORES

Protest Quartiles

First questionnaire:

	Scores included
High	32 or greater
Medium high	27-31
Medium low	21-26
Low	0-20

Second questionnaire:

	Scores included
High	14 or greater
Medium high	11-13
Medium low	9-10
Low	0-8

Third questionnaire:

	Scores included
High	33 or greater
Medium high	27-32
Medium low	21-27
Low	0-20

Protest and Sympathy Tertiles

Tertiles were used in the classification of balanced and unbalanced protest-sympathy pairs in Chapter X. The responses from Questionnaire One were divided into thirds for the inmates still in the study at Time Three.

Protest tertiles:	Scores included	Sympathy Tertiles:	Scores included
High	29 or greater	High	20 or greater
Medium	22-28	Medium	15-19
Low	0-21	Low	0-14